GOD GETS DIRTY

Consolation in the midst of Calamity

WENDY COHEN

TRILOGY

PROFESSIONAL PUBLISHING MEETS POWERFUL PROMOTION

A wholly owned subsidary of TBN

God Gets Dirty

Trilogy Christian Publishers A Wholly Owned Subsidiary of Trinity Broadcasting Network

2442 Michelle Drive Tustin, CA 92780

Rights Department, 2442 Michelle Drive, Tustin, CA 92780.

Trilogy Christian Publishing/TBN and colophon are trademarks of Trinity Broadcasting Network.

For information about special discounts for bulk purchases, please contact Trilogy Christian Publishing.

Trilogy Disclaimer: The views and content expressed in this book are those of the author and may not necessarily reflect the views and doctrine of Trilogy Christian Publishing or the Trinity Broadcasting Network.

Manufactured in the United States of America

10 9 8 7 6 5 4 3 2 1

Library of Congress Cataloging-in-Publication Data is available.

ISBN: 978-8-88738-527-3

E-ISBN: 978-8-88738-528-0

ACKNOWLEDGMENTS

To Father, Son, and Holy Spirit, thank You for giving me the idea for this book. My gratitude overflows for who You are and how You have strengthened me. Thank You for never giving up on me.

You are the Bright and Morning Star.

To my family: Your support, love, and encouragement has been invaluable. To say I'm thankful is an understatement.

To all my wonderful friends and those who've cheered me on: Bless you. I appreciate each and every one of you. I'm humbled by your interest in all that has transpired in my life.

CONTENTS

FOREWORD

A warrior is someone who has demonstrated incredible courage and intention in the pursuit of a goal.

Battlefields exist in all phases of life. I want to introduce you to a prayer warrior who serves God in many ways through the Holy Spirit by her prayer intercessions.

I first met Wendy Cohen when she was working for my company in an administrative position. Over time, I discovered her life journey and her incredible resolve in overcoming what many would call debilitating pain, due to an accident that occurred in the prime of her career as a flight attendant. Multiple failed surgeries left Wendy continuing to turn to God for reconciliation.

Wendy has personally reached out to me in prayer when she learned of my daughter's death, leaving my two small granddaughters. I know her prayer life has helped so many others in their physical and emotional journeys.

As you read this book, be prepared to examine your own journey and outreach as Wendy describes her own.

—John L Thomas
Financial consultant, business owner, and friend

INTRODUCTION

Life. What a challenge. Devastation and loss blind us to the concept that God exists. Why would He allow so much suffering in the world? The temptation of unbelief is real. Despondency wraps its invisible tentacles around the heart and suffocates expectation.

Does God care? How can we be certain?

Adversity fires its missiles at will anytime, anywhere, and toward anyone. It stands irreverent to age, economic status, nationality, gender, or belief.

Does hope exist as we navigate a maze of mayhem, chaos, and calamity? Where do we go to find it? Do we seek education? Money? Power? What effect do any of these players have on the heart and soul? The poison of sorrow and heartache begs a remedy.

Consider the notion of a Creator who knows the number of hairs on your head and thinks about you more times than the number of sand particles on the ocean shore. Would that astonish you? What if you were able to take every disturbance and burden to Him and know that He heard your cry?

Stretch your imagination and open the gate of your soul to discover a love beyond comprehension.

The overwhelming desire to share my personal experiences with Him outweigh the adversity of the task. I attest that I'm no expert. I am one who bears flaws. The remnants of ashen residue that has cloaked my existence beckons me to deliver my message.

Would that it could pour soothing oil on another's wound.

The ugly notion of giving up dangled its defeating docket in anticipation of derailing me. The snarling struggle loomed in the stormy distance. My lungs gasped for the air of supernatural vigor.

In a culture laden with social media and the pursuit of the perfect "selfie," I dare to swim upstream. The direction I choose contradicts a presentation of the polished image. Amongst these pages unfolds my private world bared for all to see. It's disheveled. No fabrication here.

Thank you in advance for allowing me to express that which has helped my journey. It's with gratitude and thanksgiving to the One who created me that I continue to carry on.

With these words I venture to impart what has brought me through.

This is my story. I hope you will join me.

CHAPTER 1
INTRODUCTION TO THE DIRT

Faith. God. What's dirt got to do with it? Let's seek it out.

First, allow me to entertain you. Recently I visited a thrift store in anticipation of finding an organizer. Out of the corner of my eye, a cute shirt grabbed my attention.

I could smell the aroma of an irresistible deal. Peering at me from a lonely rack, hung a cuddly parka.

"It's summer, what do I need a coat for?"

Its allure kept bidding me. *Try me on.*

How could I resist?

"Ooh this fits so perfectly, and it's a name brand to boot. What a find! But fifteen dollars is too much for an unneeded article."

I kept ogling it. "It's so cute. God, I want this."

Stay with me. I'll get to the dirt soon. You won't want to miss it.

Front and back, I assessed in the mirror. "No! This contradicts getting out of debt."

After much deliberation, it returned to the clerk.

"I can't afford this."

Next stop, grocery store.

A shimmering image formed in my mind. Me, on a cold winter's day, modeling my treasure for my beloved husband.

BUY ME. I KNOW YOU WANT ME.

"Enough!" I countered the nagging voice.

Inside the store a cart awaited. Once my hands grasped the handle, it happened. The brilliantly colored produce converted into furry threads.

An intercom belted out, "Don't forget to take advantage of seventy percent off attire."

My tensed fingers released their grip on the basket. I was off at warp speed.

The miraculous occured. My vehicle transformed into a heat-seeking torpedo. I morphed into a ballistic bargain-basement maniac. No turning back now. Sweat built under my arms. Panic set in.

WHAT IF?

I was a woman on a mission, frenzied for my fashion find. I was hopeful no one ran smack into the abandoned grocery buggy.

The doors seemed frozen in time. *Why is everything in slow motion? How long has it been since I left my delightful deal?*

I returned to the scene of my temptation. Saliva built in my mouth.

The unthinkable had transpired. Someone had stolen my coat!

Regardless of how many associates I inquired, it was useless.

What in the world does any of this have to do with God? And dirt? What's the connection?

Who is He? Does He care about me?

I'm not here to bring elaborate theological terms too complex to comprehend. This is a journey. I aspire to pique your imagination and explore faith for yourself.

God came down to our level, where we live. Did I lose you?

"I don't believe in God or any of that religious nonsense," you mutter.

Understood. It could be worthwhile to stick around. I reveal that God is a person and very personal. Come with me on this discovery. The choice is yours, of course. No pressure.

Dirt and God will become more acquainted through the roadmap of these pages. Interested?

The frothing-at-the-mouth jacket incidence was cause for further examination.

"God, what was that craziness about?"

Aha. He speaks.

Did you know that the God of creation is even more in pursuit of you than I was of that cozy coat? He will stop at nothing to gain your attention and draw you to Himself. Hence, He commences the chase throughout this text.

"Hogwash," you retort. Or worse.

Adversity and suffering blind our vision of a God who cares. Trust me, I'm no stranger to difficulties.

Here, on these pages, I bare my soul for all, uncertain of the response.

I concede I've been to the depths of despair. I've glared over the edge of an emotional cliff landscaped in craggy crevices. Searing affliction raged throughout my tissues and plunged me into nightmarish days of darkness.

Rather than succumbing to the inferno, I discovered a power beyond myself.

There's a great amount of trepidation to use this portrait of pain for God's glory. As I unearth the hidden details that lurk in the corners of my soul, I wonder, *Will it benefit another?*

Are you without solutions and unsure where to turn? I don't hold all the answers. I'm here to point you in the direction of comfort.

At the bright age of twenty, I gained employment with a major airline. A West Coast native, I found the move to the Big Apple was a culture shock. My youthful inventiveness served ineffective in regard to the reality of my new position. All previous notions that dreamt of a glamorous occupation fizzled. My aching feet throbbed from the lengthy twelve- to fifteen-hour days.

A month and a half later, the news of the airline's recruitment to fly the Caribbean routes perked me up. I could already hear the roar of the ocean beckoning.

I frequented many exotic islands. On the airstrip, I was able to peek out for a brief moment. Sweaty nylons clung to my legs as I plopped into the jumpseat. Back to New

York.

I pined over the prestigious landscapes in the Atlantic. I yearned to sink my toes in the sand and drink in the warmth of the sun.

Cockroach roommates greeted me in my East Coast abode. I dragged my dehydrated self up the stairs to the noisy apartment.

Three months of probation flew by, and our class was given a pass to vacation in a location of our choice. I selected Aruba. "One Happy Island" was their slogan— how perfect.

Now, this was what I'd signed up for. Three glorious days of sun and swim evaporated in a flinch. Back to the grind.

After six months, the travel passes became a close companion. Not a minute to waste. I was off to St. Croix, St. Thomas, Barbados, Aruba, St. John, to name a few. I couldn't get enough of the hot equator.

The required nine months elapsed. I transferred to Dallas, Texas. The Caribbean wasn't on the radar as regularly, but every now and then, another trip would ensue.

On one excursion to Aruba, my brother accompanied me. As an Air Force pilot, he welcomed the needed R&R.

It's remarkable that we became such proficient friends. After my arrival from the hospital as a newborn, out popped a precarious question from my brother's mouth.

"Baby sister all gone?"

He must have eventually gotten used to the idea of me.

My comrade decided a Jet Ski afternoon would be a great option.

Not for me. Like many young women, I had a vision of riding horses on the beach. I could already smell the salt-water breeze blowing through my long hair and the waves at my side.

He conceded. It was a blast—until the end of the ride.

The steady trot of the mare beneath me halted. Midair, I was thrust over her head with vigorous force. The momentum found my form splattered on the pavement. Exhaustion had taken a toll on the regal creature, and my small frame took the full impact of its weight as it collapsed on top of me.

One thousand pounds of pressure sank into my pelvis. All my years of riding horses as a youngster hadn't prepared me for this.

Horses have smarts. They amaze me.

A snort blasted from her breath as she gained force to

stand. For a second. Down she crashed once more. No getting up now.

"Get some help!" I heard in the distance.

Most of the remaining incident was a blur. The ramifications of this occurrence would become the catalyst for years of misery.

At the onset of this expedition, I was compelled to give mention and respect for any and all who have suffered. My heart and compassion for the hurting has overwhelmed me. My prayer life has gravitated to its cause.

TO EVERY ONE OF YOU, I'M DEEPLY SORRY FOR YOUR STRUGGLE.

Dirt. What is it?

You may remember as a kid making mud pies, causing excess laundry.

Food, trees, plants, and flowers receive nourishment from the soil. It is a substance that sustains us by what it produces.

I've forgotten tennis shoes when accompanying my husband on one of his construction jobs. Open-toed shoes and clay produce mucky feet.

I admit I'm not a fan of washing another's soiled extremities. But I know Someone who is.

Chapter 1: Introduction to the Dirt

This is a juncture where I interject a disputable Person of interest. At first, you may be tempted to close the book. If you determine to hang around, I purpose to give effort to make it meaningful. Grace me with your presence, if you will.

His name is Jesus.

Yes, I said it.

He is undeniably the most misunderstood man in history. But was He just a man?

My experience with Him the last thirty-plus years has been anything but boring. Exciting, yes. Difficult at points, indeed. Our interactions have held challenges, elation, laughter, heartache, and many tears. I am enthralled and mystified by Him all at once.

Jesus was well acquainted with dirt. He embarked into our world in a lowly manner. He walked in sandals on long, dusty roads. When He was born, He was placed in a manger, which equates to an animal-feeding trough. The night air reeked of smelly sheep in a nearby field. The Bible doesn't specify if He was born in a stable or a cave. Not a fancy way to be ushered into the earth.

What matters is to grapple with the reality of who He was. The God-man. He became familiar with the experience of being human.[1]

Time to slow the propellers of the plane. Your inquisition

may ask what God's humanity has to do with your reality.

Many have an opinion about the Bible that it's an ancient book, one that collects dust on a shelf. Is this truth? Why settle on the conclusion of a thing until you have researched it completely for yourself?

Words have power, meaning, and purpose. They can be instruments for help or for harm.

In a moment of intense stress, your nerves are fried. You are on the verge of a mini-breakdown. Never has a friend been more necessary. They speak the exact language to soothe. The paralyzing fear vanishes, and you regain composure.

In moments of exasperation, when I've desperately longed to hear from God, I've found an answer in His Word.

GPS has been my pal on more than one occasion. If you've lived long enough on this earth, you appreciate how convenient digital directions are. Getting lost stinks.

I define the most hairball experience as losing my way on a trip to Canada. My spouse had longed to fish in the terrain of the Canadian waters. A three-and-a-half-hour drive finalized in seven.

We left home at 9:00 a.m. to arrive in Alberta at 7:00 p.m.. After we'd had a much-needed hot meal, a snowstorm whipped up, and we couldn't see which direction to go.

The howl of the night wind, matched by a moonless sky, brought anxiety to my fatigued being. By 2:00 a.m., I determined we were lost in the forest of haunting evergreens and bears. With no GPS, I determined to pray with fervency.

God brought us through the torrent of episodes to our hotel by 4:00 a.m.

I like to refer to the Bible as my GPS, my "God-Positioning Satellite." He knows where I am. Always. He will give me direction when I ask.[2] There will be moments in life when prayer is our best ally.

As a daughter of a naval personnel, I enjoyed the opportunity to gain education regarding the military. My sibling followed in our father's footsteps to meet the status of an Air Force lieutenant colonel who served twenty years. He had the fabulous privilege of commanding those sleek F-15s. What a piece of machinery.

As much as I pleaded, the option to soar in those grandiose aircraft wasn't in the cards for me. The exterior of the spectacular specimens was my only view.

Did I mention there were plenty of cute pilots? What a blast from the past remembering those days! One of my fondest reminiscences was when my roommate and I spent the night with my brother. A lengthy game of Pictionary with his friends was on the agenda.

The small apartment was loaded with male pilots who mingled their cologne with our perfume.

My gal pal drew what appeared to be a strange blob. No one was the wiser except myself. A frog, of course!

The guys burst out in masculine laughter. I laughed so hard I noticed a strange wet feeling in my pants. Imagine my dread. Twenty-one, with a soaked bottom and surrounded by handsome young men. Were they privy to my plight?

I motioned my friend to the bathroom. She offered her jacket for a covering. Sometimes it doesn't pay to laugh that hard, but what a great get-together.

Many of my breaks involved visiting my brother. One such amazing evening at the Florida AF Base involved the unforgettable. The Eagle F-15s performed night-flying missions with afterburners.

IF YOU'VE EVER FELT THE RUMBLE OF THAT KIND OF POWER IN YOUR VEINS, THERE'S NOTHING QUITE LIKE IT.

All those adrenaline junkies lighting up the night sky is astounding.

I'm a deep thinker. I've found myself marveling how mankind can craft something as intelligent as a fighter jet. The dynamics involved in perfecting such a thing is mind-boggling. Every part has to work together in precision. When you're flying at over six Gs, you must be sure your jet is steadfast.

It's my estimation that's a small taste of how smart God is to give us the know-how to do the things we do.

Skilled surgeons perform miraculous surgeries. Scientists have discovered vital cures. Astronauts have frequented the moon.

Am I the only one, or do you agree that is off-the-charts awesome?

One can't help but ponder the enigma as to why pain is impenetrable to diagnose.

If you are a star-gazer, you can identify how vast and complex our universe is. The earth is traveling at 1,037 miles per hour.[3] The sun has to be exactly the right distance from the earth or it would fry us to a crisp. The planets are placed in pattern. How do they escape crashing into each other? *Wham!* Whoops, got off-course. My bad. It doesn't happen.

The physical specimen is something to behold. Our ligaments tie our bones together. The material needed for them to flex and stretch last an entire lifetime. The design is such that it has to meet many changing demands. That sounds suspiciously like a heavenly mathematician was involved.

Injuries strike. The substance can wear out or snap, yet it remains extraordinary in theory.

Jesus. Who is He, anyway? Due to the claims He made, there can only be a few conclusions. He said He had the power to forgive sins.[4] He stated that He and the Father (God) are one,[5] and that He was the Son of God.[6] He would be one of three things: a complete lunatic; an all-out, full-blown liar; or exactly who He said He was.

There's no force involved here. No manipulation, control, or tyranny. God doesn't need a relationship with someone who's coerced.

How many of us have ever been head-over-heels in love, only to discover the love we give isn't reciprocated? Ouch. It's no different with God. He does not want to push Himself on anyone. He extends an invitation, hoping you'll RSVP.

Have you ever been to a restaurant where it takes a lengthy spell for a greeting? Has there been an occasion when you've asked someone a question and they turned to the person next to you to answer. You felt invisible. Not a great confidence booster.

What is the method to approach God in conversation? The first stage is to acknowledge Him and that He exists. Hebrews 11:6 shares these words: "But without faith it is impossible to please Him, for he who comes to God must believe that He is, and that He is a rewarder of those who diligently seek Him" (NKJV).

My references for God come from the Bible, as well as my personal experiences with Him. The goal of this writing is to leave you with the awareness of how great His love is for you. You get to decide what to do with it.

CHAPTER 2

DIRTY RELIGION

Religion. What does it mean, exactly? What do you believe? Are you certain of its validity? The model is moral. The method is messed up.

The sacred writings are packed with stories and parables.

John records a famous passage that provides the juicy details of a religious encounter.

A lady of questionable morality is caught in the act of adultery. The angry arms that squeezed her hands shoved her at the feet of Jesus. The stiff extremists of the law held high wishes of witnessing her death by stoning. This was a common and beastly practice in ancient civilization.

Braced between two males, she convulsed. Her efforts to break free faltered. All eyes gawked at her. The temple court, where Jesus was teaching, went abuzz.

What must have been going through her mind? Frightened and ashamed, she cowered.

The self-righteous zealots were staunch fanatics of the law. They presented their case to test Jesus. Their mission was to discredit His ministry of love and grace.

The scribes and the Pharisees brought a woman caught in adultery. They set her in the center of the court and said to Him, "Teacher, this woman was caught in adultery, in the very act."[7]

Notice the Scripture states she had been caught in the "very act." Interesting. Were they passing by? Had they been tipped off? We aren't privy to those facts. Were they on the prowl to locate their next casualty?

"Jesus stooped down and wrote on the ground with His finger."[8] There has been a tremendous amount of debate about what He wrote in the dirt.

"He who is without sin among you, let him throw a stone at her first."[9]

Again, He bent down and wrote, not speaking a word.

Can you picture the scenario? Tensions are high. What will be the outcome?

The leaders were familiar with the Law of Moses. They knew right from wrong and prided themselves on being above the lowly sinners. It's speculated that Jesus might have written the sins of each of the accusers on the dusty soil. One by one, they dropped their stones and left.[10]

Straightening up, Jesus said to her, "Woman, where are they? Has no one condemned you?"[11]

"No one, Lord."[12]

This is a moment worthy of contemplation. John 3:17 says, "God did not send His Son into the world to condemn the world, but that the world through Him might be saved" (NKJV).

"Saved from what?" More on that later.

Proper attention should be attributed to His response. "I do not condemn you either. Go. From now on sin no more."[13]

I have met more people who have been hurt by religion than anything else. The uncaring pious didn't have any concern for this woman's well-being. Their issue wasn't with her. She was spicy bait in an attempt to corner Jesus and put a stop to all the wonderful miracles He was performing for the hurting and sick.

The self-righteous leaders missed the heart of the matter, and thus they missed God's heart.

Religion is a miscomprehended subject. It can be deadly if misconstrued. The casualties are too many to count. The unattainable set of standards have repelled others from God.

Scholars believe there were 613 laws that Jesus fulfilled.[14] It's important to understand your belief system and what it stands for.

The Bible is clear that not everyone who claims to stand for God is authentic at his or her core. Warnings about false prophets and teachers proliferate the Scriptures. Their motive is sheer selfish gain.[15] They exploit the truth and distort its meaning for ulterior motives.

It's imperative to know what the book says and read it for yourself to prevent deception. Followers of Christ often have differences of understanding in extracting its truths. In the process, we are to maintain kindness and consideration of one another.[16]

Relationship heals.

THE BREATH OF LIFE IS REFRESHING.

God's Spirit woos us into a life-giving relationship with Himself. How different this is from adhering to a set of rules and traditions. We will uncover more of how Jesus fulfilled all the requirements of the law for us. Think of it as owing a large sum of money and having the benefit of someone else paying your debt in full.[17]

Laws lack the power to change the heart. Obeying them is an outward sacrament of procedures that has no impact on the soul. The flipside is about a person's life, wholeness, and intimate fellowship with the One who loves them.

Religion is man's attempt to make himself right with God. The opposite involves God reaching out to us and providing the remedy to be in relationship with Him. There is a mindset involved wherein one concurs himself better than another.[18]

My first real encounter with God ensued as a teenager. As a five-year-old, I accepted Jesus into my heart. For a season, we attended church on and off as a family.

When I turned three, my dad became a heavy drinker. The midnight hour provided countless trips to my grandma's house to escape his rants. Although I didn't like it, the back of our station wagon became a familiar bed.

My brother and I squabbled and fussed with one another in the twilight hours of the "rescue wagon."

The toll my father's drinking took on each of us grew through the years. I've heard of happy drunks. That was not our situation. A harsh and angry, wild man erupted from the effect drunkenness had on him. The protective barrier he was designed to bestow was null and void. While he provided well and loved us, too many years of the polar opposite person was on the scene.

To set the synopsis for what would come later, it's important to interject an unpleasant reality. I was sexually abused by a family acquaintance at the age of eleven. I knew that if my dad found out, he could have ended up in prison due to what he'd have done to the abuser. It would be years after he died that I finally told my mom.

When I entered my teens, I wanted nothing to do with my father. My inner turmoil formed a disgust for him. He had stopped paying attention to me when I was three, so I looked to boys for my affection.

I had no idea how much emotional strain my father carried. I would later develop great compassion for him. I would soon forgive him. But the remnants of our severed union served up a damaging effect on my soul.

As a result of the separation from excessive alcohol, we no longer attended church. While my mom stayed close and active in my brothers' and my life, I still carried a void. There was a deep longing and need inside to be loved, touched, and validated.

There was a tremendous gap inside my heart. Deep down, something screamed this was abnormal. Something was missing.

I was an affectionate and family-oriented girl. The lack of having a father who was present left me vulnerable and needy.

Seventeen came with a sweet,yet rotten scenario.

Chapter 2: Dirty Religion

All the years of neglect developed into a springboard, nudging me in the direction of disaster. I got involved with a married man and was naïve enough to believe the lie that he had separated from his wife. He was thirteen years my senior, and the presence of a pseudo-father satisfied me. A desire fulfilled. For a stint.

We spent many moments together. Our romantic involvement led to discussions of marriage. Fresh out of high school, my life was busy. I was working full-time and tending to an apartment. The more we relished our companionship, the more the elephant in the room enlarged. Alcohol.

How was the evasion of departing from my childhood trauma smack in the middle of my life again?

I intensified the effort to break free from the union. The vortex of ferocious passion sucked me back in. Enraptured by the warmth of embrace, the arms of the affair tightened their clench on my substance. Inner turmoil to do the right thing gave way to my acute compulsion.

Persuasion and charm won me over. Being doted on gratified my longings. It brought temporary happiness. Though he was the instigator, the bond was mutual.

One day I reached a tipping point.

DÉJÀ VU COLONIZED MY ENVIRONMENT AND PUSHED ME OVER THE EDGE.

Morning came early as his drunken stupor kept me up into the wee hours. It might as well have been a replay of an old movie from my adolescence. The cereal box on top of the refrigerator was parked next to a liquor bottle. The body passed out on my bed was all I could take. No more. The faulty foundation of our exchange collapsed, and we parted ways.

If you or someone you know struggles with the issue of alcoholism, I know how difficult it is. My heart goes out to you. It was something my father never overcame, and it's a very distressing issue.

A family member invited me to go with her to a Bible study shortly after the romance terminated.

"Nah. Why would God want anything to do with me? What does He care, and why didn't He give me a father who was there for me?" Although I had received Jesus at the age of five, I had grown distant from Him. The grueling atmosphere at home sent me in search of fulfillment elsewhere.

Guilt and sludge enveloped my emotions, so I went. Remorse drove me to my knees. And to God. The sour awareness my path had taken before reaching the age of eighteen shocked me. I wasn't in a virtuous place.

"What can it hurt to give God a try" I resigned to the possibility it would be devoid of fun.

Perched at the foot of my mother's bed, my youthful ignorance implored of her how my future would be a pleasant one. If I surrendered completely to this God of creation, would He do something with me that I didn't like?

Those erroneous thoughts cause laughter and sadness now as I look back on my foolishness. Nothing was further from the truth. Due to the unfortunate interactions with my dad, I couldn't imagine God as a good Father. I had a skewed, warped view of Him. The idea of a loving heavenly Father who wanted a close friendship with me was foreign.

Little did I know I was on a collision course with the kindness of God, and it wrecked me. In a splendid way.

This crucial point of conversion birthed a process of forgiving my dad. I participated in counseling to release him for all offenses and disregard. Much testing transpired following my new commitment. The responsibility of healing between us was one-sided. His attitude and disdain toward me remained until I left home at the age of twenty.

False theology can be fatal. It will stop at nothing to run its exhaustive course of impossible regulations. Jesus addressed one aspect on the subject in dialogue with the Pharisees and scribes. Piety preceded their pretense. They queried Him as to why His disciples violated the tradition of handwashing passed down by the elders.[19] In return, He asked why they dishonored the commandment to honor their father and mother for the sake of their custom.[20]

Direct and to the point, His declarations enveloped the totality of the complication.

"They worship me in vain; their teachings are merely human rules."[21]

How upright does one have to be for God, anyway? The truth is, there is only One who has lived a perfect, sinless life. This belongs to Christ and Him alone.[22]

The beautiful reality of who God is displayed in that He first reached out to us. He sent Jesus, His only Son, to fulfill the law. The law was implemented to show us we could never keep it. The good news is that "Christ is the end of the Law for righteousness to everyone who believes."[23]

Are you an "everyone"?

Once I was out from under my dad's roof, he demonstrated the first signs of interest in his daughter. Since I had attained the prestigious status of flight attendant, he was now proud of me.

Performance. That's what it takes for approval? This fabricated lie permeated my walk with God for longer than I preferred. What an illustration of the fallacy of religion.

My fear and trepidation to turn myself over to God vanished. It re-formed into the most exciting journey I could have imagined. The radical transformation I experienced in my heart and behavior astounded me.

Exploration of parts of the globe ensued in my travels. What a difference from the deceit I had believed about who God was.

Is it the same for many who would consider giving God their whole self? Do you experience the anxiety that yells, "You will miss out on all the enjoyment"? Does it overrule the tugging in your soul? Is there fear involved that He may make you do things you don't want to do?

No one can guarantee what path God will take him or her if they choose to know Him. Yet it is certain that He does what is best for them. Jeremiah 29:11 encourages us with this promise to His followers: "'For I know the plans that I have for you,' declares the LORD, 'plans for prosperity and not for disaster, to give you a future and a hope" (NASB).

It's clear that life doesn't always emulate that things are manifesting for our best. How does this fit into the goodness of God? As a tapestry of yarn appears a woven mess, our circumstances often give the impression that conditions won't turn out well. This challenging area will weave itself throughout the fabric of these pages.

Parenting is a tremendous and rewarding job. The stress of raising children is outweighed by the gladness they bring to our lives. I've had the privilege of being a stepmom to a wonderful son. He has brought much delight. It gave me a greater understanding of unconditional love.

The sorrow I experienced when he made poor choices grieved me. I yearned to explain to him I could relate to his teen years. Most teenagers presume they are smarter than their elders. Like many of us, he had to learn life's lessons for himself.

I respect, love, and admire the man he has become today. And I have been twice blessed with the addition of a beautiful daughter-in-law.

God is a Father. A good one. Jesus referred to God as Father 165 times in the four gospels.[24]

What parent doesn't want the best for their kids? There were many instances when I longed for something or someone. I would pray and believe for it, yet it didn't come to pass. A wise God knew better.

Youngsters don't see that their parents own the prudence to keep them from making bad decisions. From their perspective, Mom or Dad is a killjoy. We know better.

God is no different. He sees time from beginning to end and knows the big picture.[25] It doesn't mean He always lets us know the answer. He may or may not fulfill specific requests or desires. Trust must enter the scene and comprehend He knows what's right for us.

How many parents have said to their little ones, "someday you'll thank me"?

Trust is an issue many of us face. It doesn't come with ease or overnight.

I've encountered too many individuals who have been hurt in church or damaged by religion. It's a tragedy. This false ritual at its nature is similar to a diet.

Don't you despise that word? *Diet.* All at once you switch into a ferocious carnivore on a vengeance to ravage everything in sight.

You fantasize about your next indulgence. Your mind drifts to the vision of a luscious burger that drips with cheese oozing out the sides. You can't wait to wrap your sticky fingers around the warm bun.

For myself, the notion of entertaining such a delight to ingest evoked angst. The ailment I'm contending with belies how I'm treating myself. My eating habits have been such that I consume a nourishing diet of fruits, vegetables, water, and lean meats.

IN THE FUTURE, I WOULD FORSAKE PIZZA, LASAGNA, AND ICE CREAM FOR AN ENTIRE DECADE.

The negative impact such cuisines had on my insides wasn't worth the enjoyment.

While others hosted barbecues, I was either absent

or present and feasting on next to nothing. Birthday celebrations adorned with an array of desserts and cake resulted in the same.

I passed the frosted pieces around the room. I lived vicariously through others' indulgence of the tasty morsels. Each luscious bite consumed reminded me that I dared not swallow such delicacies. The disastrous ramifications of such an option was unacceptable.

I socialized and picked up plates to make myself useful. It was important to ward off unnecessary attention to my dietary restrictions.

Statistics blare out that New Years' resolutions fail at the alarming rate of 80 pecent by the month of February.[26] Fad diets may not last, either. But when you modify the verbiage to lifestyle, something shifts. It's no longer about what you can't have, but rather about what you can. Your focus is about the variations that benefit your well-being.

We frequently balk at the word *no*. Something inside rises and urges us to go against the ruling with raving velocity. We become unhinged and bent on what we want and how we want it.

I recall a story I once heard from a pastor. He recounts this:

Two loving parents are hosting a birthday party for their small child. They invite many friends of their son, boys and girls alike. The backyard emerges into a joyous play land. The inflatable bouncy structure, small petting zoo, and games are sure to satisfy.

The dad gathers all the kids. Each face beams with anticipation.

"I want you to have fun and play all afternoon. There's only one rule you must obey. Do not spit in the flowerbed."

Giggles and squeals trail behind his lanky figure. He motions in the direction of the gorgeous, sunlit flowers.

"No spitting," he kindly commands.

With that said, he abandons the children and returns to the living room with his wife. Behind the curtain, they steady the video camera.

In threes and fours, the little nippers migrate to the flowerbed, disregarding other recreations. Clumps of saliva swirl through the air one by one. Not only did each child spit, but many chose to indulge twice. The footage of the spitting fest was sure to be a hit one day.

We crave what is off-limits. It's human nature. The parents weren't trying to spoil a lovely festivity. It was a lesson in realizing that no matter how well we have it, the appeal of the forbidden is often stronger.

Only God through Christ can set us free to have right motives and desires.[27]

Relationship with God is dissimilar to observing a set

of rules and rituals. Does one experience an amendment of character and tendencies through regulations? Is there potency in laws to repel anger? What about noxious thoughts?

Inward, lasting adaptation that pleases God can only come through a unique mode. No one will ever be noble enough on their own merit to be right with a perfect and holy God.

Consider electricity. Its source of power is available. The search for the ideal lamp has come your way. When darkness descends, your fingers click the button back and forth. Nothing.

A light bulb illuminates in your memory. You insert the plug into the socket and voilá!

Without the power to surge through the cord, a light source won't perform.

God didn't intend for us to live for Him without the proper source. Living in vital union with Him provides a fuel beyond self-effort.

When Jesus walked on this earth, He loved people. He proved it in many ways.[28] His validation of the outcast and forgotten read throughout the four gospels. A very relevant illustration of this is in the parable of the Good Samaritan.[29]

He opposed to the pious leaders. They practiced

disapproval of any deemed lesser quality than themselves. Their priorities leaned to strict adherence of handwashing and proper attire. Manmade prerequisites governed their priorities while they lacked mercy.

"God must be so pleased." They beamed with arrogant pride.[30]

Jesus wasn't impressed. He cares about the heart. His concern is for the poor, the sick, orphans, widows, and the needy.[31]

I'm astounded by a noteworthy story about a female healed on the Sabbath. This depiction portrays the ludicrous philosophy of the mindset that wounds mortals.

A woman had had a sickness caused by a spirit for eighteen years. She was bent double and could not straighten up at all.

When Jesus saw her, He called her over and said to her, "Woman, you are freed from your sickness." He laid His hands on her, and immediately she was made erect again and began glorifying God.[32]

The next part describes what transpires with the pharisaical leaders. The synagogue official was indignant because Jesus had healed on the Sabbath.

He said to the crowd, "There are six days during which work should be done; so come during them and get healed, and not on the Sabbath day."[33]

The leaders missed something extraordinary because of their mistaken view of regulations. God makes rules for our benefit, not to harm or burden us. Their twisted assessment was out of order. Their priorities were off. They missed the heart of God.

I'VE HEARD IT SAID THAT LOVE WITHOUT TRUTH IS PLAIN EMOTIONALISM, WHILE TRUTH WITHOUT LOVE IS COLD ORTHODOX.

There should be a balance of both. Truth is necessary, and love is essential. Jesus embodied grace and truth.[34]

I shook the black garbage bag.

"They're broken," I pronounced.

My spouse locked the storage door. Our belongings had been moved for the fifth time in ten years.

"I'm sorry. We'll get new ones later."

"They can't be replaced. I bought them on clearance."

He brushed the grime off his sleeveless shirt. He was ready to move on.

Not so fast, mister, I mused to myself.

The detailed metal roses that wrapped around the glass lamp bases were all that remained.

"Couldn't you have been more careful?"

"There's nothing I can do. Let's go."

Zip it. I resisted the urge to press the conundrum.

Not the end of the world, but in the temperature of the moment, clemency triumphs over damage. Even in trivial disputes, grace gives way to a better conclusion.

Something powerful jumped off the page while I was reading the Old Testament. The book of Exodus explains in detail the journey of the people of Israel through the wilderness. God instructed them to construct a mobile temple for Him to dwell among them as they traveled.[35]

This tabernacle contained the Ark of the Covenant and the Ten Commandments.[36] On top of the ark was a mercy seat. This is where God said He would meet with the priests.[37] The mercy seat was above the Ark, and the law of commandments was tucked inside.

The measurements of the Ark and the mercy seat were the exact same dimensions in width and length.[38] This was obvious in that mercy is as important as the law. God gave both for our benefit, but to have the law without mercy is heartless.

Jesus fulfilled the law, and mercy sits on top of the commandments and thus governs the law.[39]

This paints a vivid portrait of God's grace and love to people. God's wrath and anger towards mankind's decision to reject Him was satisfied in the person of Christ. When He looks at the mercy seat He remembers His covenant.[40]

CHAPTER 3

DIRTY DISTORTIONS

Labels. Most of us will have at least one or more of these if we've lived long enough. These markers don't reflect the person we are.

Grade school sets the stage for some of the most degrading insignias. Who doesn't recall overhearing the calls of "four eyes," "skinny," "geek," "dumb ,"or "nerd"? These false identifiers shout in our faces. They form a forceful coercion to align with their accusations.

The obligation to cut them down at the root requires diligence. Their propaganda can raid our adult lives. We must resist.

Interviews are one of the places these dirty devils pop up uninvited. I enjoyed the movie *The Pursuit of Happyness.*[41] The main character surges through the door in grungy jeans and a T-shirt for an imperative interview. His circumstances had plummeted. On the day when it counted, everything went south.

His drive and determination propelled him forward in spite of his shaggy appearance. Now, that's overcoming.

Is there remediation for the nasty intruders wandering inside our heads? What about those from outside sources?

God desires that each of us would have a strong identity that comes from knowing how valuable we are to Him. PhotoShopped magazine covers and illustrious images strike a chord about our shortcomings. These are not confidence boosters.

Not one person who has walked the planet has shared the same fingerprint. What a strong case for individuality.

When heartache busts down our gate, it's critical to receive comfort from someone who relates. How discouraging to expound a disturbing experience, only to recognize the hearer is clueless.

I'm an advocate for great counseling. I've invested much energy working through my childhood trauma. The memories that remain are no longer an open wound. They are scars that tell a story.

Did you know Jesus bears scars?

Matthew is the first book of the New Testament. Jesus' ministry commenced when He reached the age of thirty.[42] His interactions with prostitutes, adulterers, and tax collectors are recorded in the Scriptures. He came to free mankind from the chains that bind us. These are not physical chains, but rather shackles of the mind that trap us and prevent us from living with assurance.

I've said on many occasions He came to save me from myself.

ARMS OUTSTRETCHED, THE ESSENCE OF DEITY SPILLED TO THE GROUND WITH EACH DROP OF BLOOD.

Although He was nailed to a Roman cross with hands and feet pierced by iron spikes,[43] it was His love that held Him there. Added to this barbaric torture was a beating and scourging that ripped the flesh clean off His body. The whips unleashed their fury on the perfect Son of God. In His most agonizing hour, the people spit on Him, pulled His beard, and mocked Him.[44]

With every blow of the metal scraps that dug into His tissue, you and I were in His thoughts.

As His battered body hung on the cross, He uttered a piercing statement: "Father, forgive them; for they do not know not what they are doing."[45]

Incredible.

Most of us can't imagine the humiliation of such a cruel act in our modern world.

Jesus can identify with all the sorrow we endure. Who better to define us and relabel us than the One who went through the worst of the world's hellish treatment?

Every summer, when August rolled around, my excitement for the county fair heightened. The whiffs of cotton candy and baked pretzels stirred my stomach. The squeals afar beckoned my presence. The endless trips on the roller coasters fulfilled my childhood thrills. My friends and I spent the entire day and night at the fair, hoping it would never end.

We snickered as we stood in front of the distorted mirrors in the funhouse, poking fun at each other. Our girlish figures became weird and dorky.

Fast-forwarad to today. Do we peer at the reflection staring back and gauge our self-worth on what we behold? We tend to judge ourselves by our looks, hair, clothing, and whatever else that seems principal.

If we have curly hair, we want straight. If we're short, we may wish we were taller. On and on it goes.

Shame distorts and gnaws at our core. It reminds us we aren't who we ought to be. It's easier to mask our blemishes than to uncover defects. The risk for disapproval is too high.

When Jesus died on the cross, He took our disgrace, and in return, He endows us identity and worth.[46]

We are made in the image of God.[47] Proud parents melt when they gaze into the faces of their newborn infants.

When a friend or relative comments they look like Mom or Dad, it furthers their wonder. And why not? They share the same DNA.

We also have the same DNA as God, so to speak. We are not equal to Him, but we are made in His image.[48]

When we know who we are, we can reflect His nature, which is good.[49] It's imperative to grasp who He is and what He thinks about us.

I was quite unexperienced early in my career and in my move to New York City. Immediately I was assigned an employee number, which remained throughout my entire profession. Much revolved around this figure. Purchasing uniforms, getting paid, and signing in for a trip required the allocated digits.

Staying afloat in the classification of numeric identification takes exertion. Uniqueness is zapped away without it. Mathematical equations do not recognize eye color, likes and dislikes, or favorite restaurants. Deflating.

I repelled at the idea of being a cookie-cutter attendant in a blue polyester uniform. After all, we looked alike in that sense.

The desire for uniqueness is universal. Piercings, tattoos, and choice of cloaking beg recognition. But only one version of ourselves exists.

WHEN GOD MADE EACH OF US, HE THREW AWAY THE MOLD.

You and I will never be a carbon copy of anyone else.

What bigger boost of self-esteem is there?

God didn't make us clones or robots. How boring that would be! We each have the freedom to express our unique taste in varied forms.

The health challenges I faced led me down a contorted road of deep insecurity. Nine months of probation passed, and I was off to the southern state of Texas.

Snuggled in my bed after midnight, a sharp, shooting pain clenched my groin. I shot out of bed from my slumber. The concern of the unknown gripped me more than the painful sensation itself.

The ring from the phone jolted my parents out of their dozing. A late-night call doesn't usually spell good news.

Little time passed before my admission to the hospital for surgery number one. An inguinal hernia was discovered, more often experienced in males than in females.[50]

Diagnosis complete, and abdomen closed up. No remedy yet.

Oh, to have possessed the ability to look forward to the next thirty years. I would never have capitulated to the upcoming procedures. Hindsight is always 20/20. Black and white descriptions of misdiagnoses didn't capture my agony. The myriad of unseen issues whirling about inside me puzzled my thoughts.

Rejection is damaging. Convoluted dissertations in medical settings left me with the intuit I wasn't always heard.

Jesus understands. He came to His own, and those who were His own did not receive Him.[51] He, too, experienced the scorn of those who ridiculed and belittled Him.

Imagine planning a surprise visit to a long-lost relative. You purchase choice gifts with yearnings of reconciliation. Your hands tremble as they reach for the relative's doorbell. Your smile reaches from ear to ear. It quickly dissipates as the door is slammed in your face.

God experiences this constantly. Sad. He craves to come in and fellowship with us, for us to receive His Son as the remediation for our severed relations.

The concept of Jesus being a human is supernatural. It's unattainable for the natural mind.

The amount of films dedicated to superheroes and mystic phenomenon are plentiful. It's beyond cinematic to ponder life outside our limited sphere of this planet. The fantasy of unparalleled power and other death-defying feats garners our attention.

Is it so far-fetched to believe there could be a real God in the universe who is a supernatural Being?

I've plummeted to the depths of despondency and reached for His hand when I didn't want to hold on to anything. I didn't like to admit I was upset with Him in certain instances. After all, He's God, isn't He? Why doesn't He just fix everything? If only it were so simple.

Do you fall into the category of having it all together and not seeing your need for help? Then you may not find anything of value here. But if you find yourself on the other side of the fence broken and fragmented, then this is great news.

GOD WANTS—NO, GOD LONGS—TO GIVE HIS LOVE TO YOU.

In an unconditional way.[52] He yearns to have friendship with you at the deepest part of your being.[53] This kind of security is priceless. Most everything else is unpredictable.

Dare to gaze into perfection and see yourself the way you were made. You are one who has infinite and eternal value separated from a marred perception. God gives us this gift through Jesus.

There is no disfigurement, no distortion, no confusion in Him. He is only majestic beauty and glory.[54] Will you allow Him to shine on your mortal existence and raise you out of the muck and mire?

People, cars, and appliances fail. Houses and relationships crumble. Dreams fade, and mankind passes on to death. Animals die. Oh, how far from the original plan of existence God intended.

Genesis 1:26 tells us, "Then God said, 'Let Us make mankind in Our image, according to Our likeness; and let them rule over the fish of the sea and over the birds of the sky and over the livestock and over all the earth, and over every crawling thing that crawls on the earth" (NASB).

God created us to have dominion and rule, not as tyrants, but to live in harmony with creation and with each other.

"God saw all that he had made, and it was very good."[55]

Note that it didn't say "good"; it said "very good." This brings the distortion question to the forefront: If God is so trustworthy, then why is there so much heartache and evil in the world?

Don't most all the superhero genres have an enemy? Indeed. As do we. He is slimy enough to drape the veil over us. He masks his ugly schemes so we will disregard his actuality. Dare we go there?

Wrestle with the fact that even in the presence of an upright God, trouble still exists. From where does it originate?

We've probed into distortions and religion. We're on the

cusp of exploring a wicked force that conspires against us. Much like a competent mystery, the adversary intertwines fabricated evidence to frame God. The outcome? Fear: *False Evidence Appearing Real.*

If successful, he has won the case. He can now propel our allegiance in the opposite direction of an impeccable heavenly Father.

Only when one knows the nature and character of something can they trust it. We will return to the discussion on virtue versus evil later.

Catastrophe and trauma will send us speeding off the runway if we don't keep it in check. The natural and immediate reaction assumes God doesn't care.

God has blessed us with many benefits, one of them being freewill. The privilege carries responsibility and accountability. Our radar tells us that if God loves us, bad things wouldn't transpire. This mentality lacks a vital component, namely that there are other passengers who affect our travels in this life, not to mention the vile forces at work.

If our hearts remain steadfast upon God and His promises, it's not as easy for our attitude to be highjacked. The gutter of despondency shrieks from the abyss. Persistent, bulldogish faith must be activated for success.

Where are God's promises found? In the Bible. How do you understand it? A delay has been set for this part of our adventure.

This script of God is His love letter. It also behaves as a reflection, to show us where we've fallen short. Not so fun. Romans takes the reader in deeper detail concerning grace and the law. Romans 5:20 states that the law came in so that the transgression (sin) would increase, but where sin increased, grace abounded all the more.

The Gospel is Good News because Jesus came to fulfill the law where we were unable to do so.[56] Its purpose was to bring us to a place of wakefulness, understanding that we have fallen short of God's standard. Now we can receive His remedy of forgiveness and salvation.[57]

"You read my mail," is a familiar phrase.

A beautiful revelation of grace sparkled across the page. It was as if God had, indeed, read my mail. I groaned with desire to be loosed from striving and to know His mercy in greater depth.

He spoke so clearly: *Look into the mirror of grace.*

Our failures and shortcomings were atoned for on the cross.

See yourself as a candidate for God's love, acceptance, and forgiveness through Christ. It will alter the direction of your days.

CHAPTER 4
DIRTY DISAPPOINTMENTS

Bankruptcy. Not a pretty word. Been there, done that.

We are much more than our fiascos. Aren't we?

Of course we are. Do we really deem it is so and walk in such a manner?

COVID-19 is proof things can change in an instant. Natural disasters, job loss, or financial ruin can torch our cocoon in an instant.

Divorce, a health crisis, or the passing of a loved one turns our world inside out.

Do you pull up your bootstraps and suck it up? Does sheer determination provide the fuel you need to navigate misfortune?

Flashback to a physician's office. A second operation was required to repair the hernia.

I'm only in my early twenties! My mind yelps at the blunder of this senseless mess.

"You're lying," almost tumbles off my tongue.

I wanted nothing to do with any of this. I should be working and enjoying my vocation as a flight attendant.

Unseen, internal torture that ransacks the nourishment of a body is blind to the visible eye. Hernia procedures are commonplace for most people. I must have had the intuition it would have a drastic impact on my future. The process used in the 1990s was more dinosaur in nature.

Although reluctant, I forged ahead, based on the medical advice I'd been given. All desire of a quick resolution mutated into a nightmare experience.

The root diagnosis would not come for another twenty-seven years. This was just the beginning.

A spider spins its web and weaves an intricate design difficult to follow. The twists and turns ahead for me were as capricious as the fine threads of the aphid's network.

The day preceding Thanksgiving found me discharged and sent home. I sprawled around the base of the commode, drained from violent projections.

The next several years copied a merry-go-round. Doctor visits, tests, procedures, scans, exams, and X-rays kept me running. The medical bills toppled off the edge of the table.

I was on the cusp of what would become an emotional and mental inferno in the impending future.

My anatomy was in a perpetual state of a stimulated sympathetic nervous system. This malady is branded as "fight or flight."

I stayed close to God and His Word, yet I knew nothing about how to claim healing verses for myself. I had the firm belief God was more than able to heal me, but at that point, all I knew was to seek help from the medical professionals.

It's okay to have questions, to ponder the meaning of things. But what if everywhere you turn, the answers evade?

You may have been an excellent spouse and still suffered divorce. If you were laid off and gave your all to your employer, it stings.

SOMETIMES LIFE ISN'T FAIR, AND WE WANT ANSWERS.

I'm taking you with me where I was wounded. I had the same doubts and questions and sought His counsel.

Grappling with the curveballs in our private world is drizzled with turmoil and struggle.

God isn't on our timetable, I have discovered. But I will say that through perseverance and persistence, we find Him when we seek Him with all our hearts.[58]

I refused to settle for anything less than real, tangible solutions. I had to seek Someone who had experienced misery and travail so He could relate to me. That's what I found in Jesus, the suffering Messiah.[59]

Jesus bore more anguish than we can fathom. The difference is, He didn't have to. He chose to—huge disparity here. And why? Why would He choose to die? That is the question of worthy of exploration.

His tenaciousness under pressure amazes me. Immersed in the pages of the sacred volume of text, I envision Him as cool as a cucumber as He responds to His critics.

Plenty of exciting destinations ensued with my brother. Despite the ailments progressing in my condition, I seized the opportunities. We ventured to the island of Barbados. Burrowed amongst the isles of the sapphire Caribbean, it was a favorite.

My memory today is vivid as I recall the deep need for laughter at the moment.

We hailed a taxi at the airport. I inquired of the driver about the fare. His response sparked a laughable dispute.

I reminded him it used to be a lesser amount a few years before, to which he replied, "'Used to be' was a long time ago."

My brother got such a kick out of this statement. We joked about it for years and made it into a one-word statement. It went like this: *usedtobewasalongtomago.*

Every now and then, we encountered an increase in cost on a given excursion. We squared off and quoted, "*Usedtobewasalongtomago.*"

Back to a more important question: Was Jesus human, and if so, why was it necessary? Was He, too, disappointed? Did He ever face feelings of discouragement?

He subjected Himself to the very elements He had created.

Did His cheeks turn rosy at the discharge of wind on His face? Did He marvel at the intricate drawings on the wings of the butterfly that He Himself had crafted?

Hebrews 4:15 explains: "For we do not have a high priest who cannot sympathize with our weaknesses, but One who has been tempted in all things just as we are, yet without sin" (NASB).

He also experienced woe, hunger, and fatigue.

Performance reviews can evoke anxiety. What if you are handed a less-than-favorable report by your superior? To top it off, what if you discover they have zero experience with your assigned duties?

What person would see a physician if the doctor hadn't graduated from medical school?

A professional is only as accomplished as his knowledge, skill set, and experience.

How comforting to know the Lord took on skin and walked among us.[60] He is able to identify with us, and that makes Him ever so able to help in our hour of need.

How can we say that God doesn't understand us when He was one of us? Jesus was God in the flesh.

Most have heard of Mary and the virgin birth. This is a mystery.[61]

When sin entered the world through man, it required a payment, one we were unable to meet. Jesus endured the same trials we face, yet He was without sin.[62] Without His humanity, the substitute would have been insufficient.

Liken the liability as an enormous calculation that would take more than a lifetime to pay, then in strides a billionaire who provides the funds and cancels the bill.

Many pastors and scholars deem that all our questions will be answered in heaven, or that by then, it won't matter. But what about now?

These are extraordinary days. Wildfires, tornadoes, hurricanes, tsunamis, disease, and death are prevalent. Is there anything beyond this life? We live, eat, work, marry, play, and perish. Have you ever given thought to where you will go when you die?

What options exist to ward off the trajectories that come our way? Does a clenched fist loaded with rage suffice? Doubtful.

I love roller coasters. The excitement of the next twist brings a level of thrill unmatched by anything else. However, an emotional roller coaster that leaves your functionality on the floor isn't worth the ride. Lasting glee would take root in my future. I also attribute joy as this: Jesus overcomes yuckiness.

Negative feelings threatened to flatten me. It wasn't attractive.

ANXIETY, DISCOURAGEMENT, AND DEPRESSION SHOWED UP WITH THEIR BAGS OF BRICKS.

Their aim was to sideline me, to take me down for the count. Spiritual maturity was my pursuit. These unwanted invaders demanded sweat and tears.

A physical and psychological squall brewed. I was trapped in the heat of biological and chemical chaos. At certain intervals, conversations at work sent me straight to the restroom to hide the hot tears burning my cheeks. Exhaustion and a severe lack of sleep left me with few coping skills.

I did a stellar job icing the injured cake with self-criticism.

"What's wrong with you?" I shouted at the mirror.

I lacked understanding and knowledge of all that was materializing inside me.

The sensation of a large metal clamp squeezing the delicate tissue of my entrails was a daily episode. Apprehension to ingest meals intensified. The searing jabs at 3:00 a.m. weren't worth the cost. I relinquished the idea now and again.

My social life became sparse. Work, family, and church required my attention and left me with only fragments of energy to spend.

When petitioned, my family members would divulge the details of my dilemma. A surprise reaction ensued. Most claimed they would have never known. I put forth great determination to maintain a pleasant demeanor. I found solace in being a delightful presence. The exterior of my disposition was in opposition to the interior hindrance.

WHEN TRIALS HIT, AN INTERNAL BATTLE DICTATES THAT THE NARRATIVE OF OUR LIFE SHOULD PLAY OUT DIFFERENTLY.

I like to say I have an audience of one. Not that it doesn't matter how we project ourselves, but shouldn't the nitty-gritty be what God thinks of us?

Relationships are wonderful if they're healthy and positive. Strife and tumult is anything but pleasant. Wouldn't it be sublime to have a deep, fulfilling relationship with one you could always count on? There's security in being with someone who is explicitly trustworthy. I have found God to be that Person for me.

By no means have I always received what I've wanted. Situations consistently do not fashion themselves as planned. Yet the constant assurance in Him keeps me grounded. My wheels may come loose, but at least they don't fly off in every direction.

Jesus walked the earth for thirty-three years in a physical body. He chose twelve men to be His closest companions, known as the disciples. The New Testament was authored in the Greek language. It has since been translated into English and many other languages around the world. The original word for "disciples" in the Greek is *mathetes*. This is another word for "somebody who engages in learning through instruction."[63]

I love this group of motley men. They give me hope. Their perpetual bumblings and stumblings tells us we don't have to be perfect. From a more sophisticated perspective, they were everyday, average guys. Once they followed the path of the Messiah, their focus reallocated forever.

The four gospels—Matthew, Mark, Luke, and John—depict the era of Christ on earth. Many accounts of His miracles, good deeds, and instruction are recorded. He was named Rabbi, meaning "teacher."[64]

Disappointment hit the apostles' doorstep, as well. They held belief that the promised Messiah was going to set up His Kingdom on the earth. The path of the cross wasn't on their agenda. It threw them for a loop. The Roman government was oppressive. They longed for a new leader.[65]

What does this have to do with our twenty-first-century existence?

These men had close contact with Jesus. They walked, served, and ate with Him. Questions ensued, and issues were brought to the table. They weren't immune to letdowns.

We aren't promised utopia here on this earth, but we have One who will protect our souls while we are in the valley of despair.[66]

In John 14:8, Philip said to Jesus, "Lord, show us the Father and it is enough for us" (NASB).

Jesus replied, "Have I been with you for so long a time, and yet you have not come to know Me, Philip? The one who has seen me has seen the Father; how can you say, 'Show us the Father'?"[67] Do you not believe that I am in the Father, and the Father is in me?"[68]

Jesus was stating that He represents God completely in a tangible form.

For some, the idea that God is three individuals—Father, Son, and Holy Spirit—just doesn't compute.[69]

During my season as a Sunday school teacher, the inquiry of God's nature required explanation. The illustration I chose was to hold up three fingers and turn them sideways. Three in one.

This story is worthy of acknowledgment.

A teacher was doing her best to explain the Holy Spirit to her class. She held up a large pretzel and pointed out three holes. She asked the young lad to recite back what he had learned.

He grabbed hold of the pretzel. "The first hole is the Father, the second one is Jesus, and the third hole is the Holy Smoke."

Got to love that!

God requests a relationship with us. He is passionate in His love for us and is interested in being our Friend.[70] He provided an instruction manual known as the Bible to help us get to know Him and His ways.

PEACE ISN'T THE ABSENCE OF CONFLICT. IT'S THE ABILITY TO FUNCTION IN THE MIDST OF DIFFICULT SITUATIONS.

Jesus provides His peace when we belong to Him.[71]

CHAPTER 5

DOES DIRTY MEAN DUMB?

"No duh." An eighties phrase. Still humorous.

Who would elect themselves to appear dumb?

Earning an undergraduate degree is an exceptional achievement.

I am the sibling of an intelligent individual who holds five Top Gun awards as an F-15 fighter pilot.

He added a prestigious PhD to his repertoire, as well.

When we were kids, I accused him of highjacking the brains in the family. He claimed I stole the looks. All in fun, of course.

I have abundant respect for his accomplishments. He worked very hard to achieve them.

How do we merge faith in an unseen God, an ancient manuscript, and smarts? Can they coexist?

There are vast resources available about historical facts that bolster our faith in God: *Evidence That Demands a Verdict* by Josh McDowell; *The Case for Christ* by Lee Strobel; and the material found at www.patternsofevidence.com are merely a few.

Previous atheists have asked the hard questions. The highly esteemed scientist Dr. Hugh Ross has written many books. He delves into the understanding of science and God.

The next season of medical havoc produced more frustration in my life. A marathon of new physicians, tests, scans, procedures, and drugs landscaped my subsistence.

It didn't make sense. Hernia surgery is commonplace. How had my ecosphere turned inside out from a course of action so ordinary? The top blew off, and the sides toppled over. Nothing was the same. This mysterious stinging didn't line up with any simple remedy.

"I despise these walls. Stark white. They're all the same."

Accumulated trips to the practitioner's office grew old.

Bumping into dividers, vertigo, confusion, and other unwanted side effects plagued my existence. Pill after pill I swallowed, believing the report that they would help.

I awoke to saturated sheets and pillows, snatched the medication, and tossed it across the room.

In a stupor of drug delirium, I traipsed to the bathroom yet again. A strange pressure on my bladder sent me to the restroom every hour during the day. Sometimes more. This intruder stole more and more time.

A third operation came. I prepared for a possible resection of the colon. I continued to place assurance in the doctors' expertise. A number of adhesions were taken down, only to reappear in subsequent procedures.

With each surgical process, I yearned to wake up brand-new and painfree. With each failure to achieve the expected result, my emotions unraveled.

"Shouldn't I be doing something phenomenal at twenty-eight? Not this," I groaned.

Most physicians are wonderful people who work hard to help their patients. They, too, are people and do not always own every answer.

It would be years before I was aware of the teaching on faith for healing. I still hold gratitude for all the caring surgeons and experts who tried.

WE ARE GOD'S EXQUISITE WORKS OF ART.[72]

I have studied basic anatomy. In doing so, I discovered how ingeniously created our bodies are. They are spectacular and cry out the existence of an intelligent Creator.

Our bodies contain blood vessels, arteries, muscles, organs, tissue, and bones. There are around seven hundred skeletal muscles[73] and 206 bones[74] in the body. The heart, lungs, and brain are vital organs and complex. One small error in any of these major players would be life-threatening. They work together in proper array without any contribution on our part.

Wherein is the disconnect that we are an original design by a Creator?

Small airports with ramp stands are rare. Decades ago, they were more customary.

Once in a while, I found myself daydreaming on these stairs. The sleek, panoramic view of a silver fuselage fascinated me. I would quiz my brother on aerodynamics. His expertise qualified his answers.

Boy, do those F-15s tear up the sky.

I CRINGED WHILE HIS CHEEKS BLEW UP BEYOND PROPORTION PULLING 8 G'S.

His forte under pressure in the centrifuge was palpable. I gave thought to the forte our bodies possess.[75]

Where does the capability to do such wonders originate?

The brain is a very intricate computer.

Trips to the moon, organ transplants, and other feats of

wonder should snag our assiduity. As the miracles of these facts play out every day, do we appreciate their mystery and source?

A famous evangelist wisely said, "I've never understood how a brown cow can eat green grass and make white milk."

God is faithful to answer many of our questions in the Scriptures. Some things aren't recorded there because we have been given the freedom to decide. He did give us a brain, after all.

Some would argue that the Bible couldn't be true as the authors are no longer alive. Permit me to counter with the proposed consideration.

I enjoy the arts. My husband has blessed me with gratification to savor ballets, operas, and several local plays.

Shakespeare lived in the 1500s and authored many works. I have never met him, nor have any of us living in the twenty-first century. His writings are evidence of his life. There remains no question of this fact. Why, then, the unremitting challenge of the validity of Scripture?

The writers of the Bible wrote their accounts during the epoch they were alive. The disciples were eyewitnesses of the life of Christ on earth. Inspired by God, they wrote about how everything unfolded.[76]

There is much in this holy publication on relationships and how to get along with one another. There's a movement of kindness taking place, and there's much about that topic in Scripture, as well.

"The Lord is compassionate and gracious, slow to anger and abounding in mercy."[77]

"Answer me, Lord, for Your mercy is good; according to the greatness of Your compassion, turn to me."[78]

"In order that in the coming ages he might show the incomparable riches of his grace, expressed in his kindness to us in Christ Jesus."[79]

"Be kind to one another, tender-hearted, forgiving each other, just as God in Christ also has forgiven you."[80]

God loves to rescue us.[81] Jesus has bridged the gap between sinful man and a holy God. Salvation is well-explained in Romans 10:9–10.[82]

Soft feathers, big personalities, and pleasant chirps delight my senses. I adore birds. Two peach-faced lovebirds stole my heart. Each lived eleven years. Too short. They both have passed, but their memory is freshly alive in my mind. I've rescued a handful of these flying creatures through the years. One setting stands out.

Mice had populated the surrounding area. To ensure they didn't burrow in the cars, we set out glue traps. Not a method for future use.

Chapter 5: Does Dirty Mean Dumb?

Our eyes met when I turned in the direction of movement. A frightened scrub jay was stuck in a glue trap. I leapt into action and tugged its feet from the goo.

Distress shifted to relief. I sensed the gratitude in its helpless gaze. We bonded immediately. Still, there was work to do.

The jar of mayonnaise was of great value. I greased its legs, removing the sticky debris. It responded to the effort.

In an instant, my new friend liberated itself.

The course it chose affected many landing spaces in the room. Little blobs of mayo dripped off my décor.

After a bout of stress, I prayed, and the creature landed, minus several tailfeathers. I scooped it up and finished my task.

It rested quietly inside the empty cage with blueberries and water.

The next day I located a wild bird rescue facility within a forty-five-minute drive.

A couple months passed, and I received a call from the rescue organization. It was at a juncture when I could pick up the critter and return it to its native habitat.

What a thrill to open the box and watch it fly away. Exhilarating.

WHATEVER RUIN IN WHICH WE FIND OURSELVES, GOD CARES.

He came to give us life and freedom.[83] It must overjoy His heart to come to our aid when we're in a sticky mess.

Rescued doesn't state the irreverence for personal responsibility. There are stages when He wants us to learn from our mistakes. Some decisions have consequences. Yet He is so forgiving and merciful, and He wants to help us.[84]

Do you have to check your brain at the entrance when considering coming to faith in God? No. Your brain and mind aren't left out of the equation.

We exercise faith daily by sitting in a chair, driving, and simply breathing the air. Our full understanding isn't required for us to do so, nor is it when reading God's Word.

Things can get violently distorted in our world. There are many illusions, representations, and portrayals of God. Too many are a complete façade.

Arizona was a state frequented in my travels. On one particular visit, while I was driving back to the airport, a furious sandstorm whipped up. Tumbleweeds spun in the air like tiny tornadoes. Hues of amber gold permeated the atmosphere. A sketchy outline of a white vehicle was the single visibility. I clung to the image during the grisly ordeal. Thirty minutes seemed like an hour.

What obstacles inhabit your mind that obstruct your view of God? If we attempt to access Him using only our five senses, it will bring confusion. Wisdom says to ask of Him and seek His ways for truth.[85]

THERE'S A DECEPTION THAT WHAT IS NOT VISIBLE ISN'T REAL. THERE'S A LOT MORE TO OUR WORLD THAN WHAT WE SEE AND FEEL.

CHAPTER 6
DIRTY DECISIONS

Decisions, decisions.

Hundreds of variations vie for our consideration.

Whom should we marry? What occupation best suits us? What brand of cell phone and provider is the optimal best? What house should we buy? Can we afford a new automobile, or is a used version reliable?

A major decision drew my thoughtfulness that could sway the trajectory of my future.

A fourth operation ensued. My resolve to locate agreeable menu items shriveled. A large clump of scar tissue developed in my groin from incisions. My pelvis was sliced, scraped, and explored.

Burning, gnawing, pinching affliction seized my colon and suffocated the life out of me. This condition gained a nasty name termed "chronic." Too familiar became the torture experienced at 3:00 a.m. I tossed and turned, threw off the covers, and paced the floor. Fatigue, medication hangovers, and lack of sleep shoved me to my knees.

I forged ahead in pursuit of specialists in many different states. Pricy alternative therapies racked up a hefty bill.

During difficult treatments, I found joy in sharing God with others. Compassion welled up inside my heart for the sorrows and suffering others endured.

While visiting a specialist in California, I received another injection. I sized up the lengthy needle. I had met many of them, but we never became friends.

"Please be nice," I asserted.

"Ah, no such fortune."

Brothers love to tease.

"Are you a sprinkler when you drink water?"

My mom had accompanied me on this trip. Bronchitis decided to grace me with its presence. Flat-out miserable. Full of holes and a nasty cough to go with it. I remained hopeful anyway.

The expert advice given at this appointment was to catch a flight from San Francisco to Los Angeles. There, I would encounter another expert who might do better. Off we went.

"Let's do it," I replied later at the new physician's advice.

A hush ensued.

"I'd rather have the three nerves clipped than live like this," I broke into his reticence.

"THERE'S A DOWNSIDE. YOU WILL NO LONGER HAVE SEXUAL FUNCTION."

No hesitation. If marriage was on the radar down the road, I would deal with the ramifications at that time. I had experienced a failed marriage in my early thirties and was celibate at that point.

The date was set. Regardless of the sacrifice, I focused on the prize: relief.

Faith is tested when a decision of magnitude is required. Especially when the outcome is unknown.

In Genesis, the first book of the Old Testament, chapter 2:8 states, "The LORD God planted a garden toward the east, in Eden; and there He placed the man whom He had formed."

Who hasn't heard of the Garden of Eden? Paradise. Everything was perfect. There was one catch. A choice. From all appearances, it seemed harmless. After all, produce is advantageous for us, is it not?

This was not a trite piece of fruit. It held a decision

that would alter the course of man's destiny. The tree held power. This timber was named the Tree of the Knowledge of Good and Evil.[86] Temptation shimmered its delightful deceit.

"Eat. You will be like God."[87]

Amongst the lush foliage lurked a shrouded secret. The evil opponent to man's soul disguised himself in light.[88]

Why would God tolerate such a thing? It is the glory and beauty of God's goodness to His created beings: free will. True liberty can't exist without opposition.

We've heard it said you can't have sunny days without the rainy ones. So it goes with the power to choose.

Adam and Eve stared into the lie and conceded.[89]

Choices and consequences. I've never forgotten that phrase. I racked up a few traffic tickets in my thirties. Rather than pay an increase in insurance, I opted for the defensive driving course.

The videos were stark reminders of injurious accidents. The instructor drove the point home. They can be avoided.

Every day we make small and sometimes large decisions. Some of them have no real backlash, while others can pose problems if not taken seriously.

Compromise costs. This single act in the Garden trickled its effects throughout man's history.

What exactly played out in this lush green habitat?

The perfect man and woman shared their environment with a snake. This was no ordinary reptile.

"Now the serpent was more crafty than any beast of the field which the LORD God had made. And he said to the woman, 'Indeed, has God said, "You shall not eat from any tree of the garden?"'"[90]

This un-proverbial tête-à-tête ensued.

"The woman said to the serpent, 'From the fruit of the trees of the garden we may eat; but from the fruit of the tree which is in the middle of the garden, God has said, "You shall not eat from it or touch it, or you will die."'"[91]

WHOA! BACK THE BUS UP.

You're trying to tell me a snake spoke?

This entity is further described in progression.

Let's dive deeper into the phenomenon.

More inviting dialogue takes place from the convincing viper.

"The serpent said to the woman, 'You surely will not die! For God knows that in the day you eat from it your eyes will be opened, and you will be like God, knowing good and evil.'"[92]

God had spoken His plan. The ophidian had given an

opposing argument. It was up to the couple to decide which voice to accept as true and act upon.

This plot plan doesn't embody a new idea. The contention that builds in a cinematic scene gives illustration to it. The hero has a challenge to overcome, while the enemy of the main character has a strategy to thwart his success.

The method to know God is similar to the way we become acquainted with another person. You spend time with them and get to know what they like and dislike. Their dreams and passions become important to us. God is found through His Word, *the Bible*, through prayer and immersing ourselves in His presence.

The Almighty had spoken His instructions. Nothing was off-limits except for the Tree of the Knowledge of Good and Evil.[93]

Recall the spitting fest?

Did they find satisfaction in all the other saplings and animals provided? Of course not. They migrated to the prohibited.

God extends His best and lets us determine the outcome. Right off the bat, He presented the option to be for Him or to reject Him. I can't say I blame Him. Love that isn't voluntary isn't love at all.

Once again, the topic of the verbal snake arises. This could be a place where many say, "I've heard enough!"

It is strange, to say the least. In a future chapter, there will be more about this creature that spoke, although it is an odd thing. Keep in mind this demonic creature was wrapped in a snakeskin.

Up until now, we don't know what the interval was between perfection and the new twist of events.

"When the woman saw that the tree was good for food, and that it was a delight to the eyes, and that the tree was desirable to make one wise, she took from its fruit and ate; and she gave also to her husband with her, and he ate."[94]

"Then the eyes of both of them were opened, and they knew that they were naked; and they sewed fig leaves together and made themselves loin coverings."[95]

One of my dear friends sent me a excerpt worth mentioning.

A little boy opened the big family Bible. He was fascinated as he fingered through the old pages. Something fell out of the book. He picked up the object and looked at it. It was a timeworn leaf that had been pressed between the pages.

"Mama, look what I found," the boy called out.

"What have you got there, dear?"

With astonishment, the young boy answered, "I think it's Adam's underwear!"

The rest of the account of what transpires is found in Genesis 3:8–24.

God wasn't happy. For many years, I pondered this story. It wasn't until a very wise preacher pointed something out that it resonated.

God knew if they remained in the Garden they would have also eaten from the Tree of Life.[96]

If they had continued in the state they were, there would never have been the option to later redeem them. The status of their souls was now tainted. God couldn't leave humanity in this condition to exist there for eternity.

It was out of God's love for man that He prevented an additional opportunity for mankind to cause himself more damage. Who would want to live in a marred state forever?

God is wise enough to know we need direction and guidance to make proper judgments. Any parent would want the same for their growing children.

"All I did was knock over the glass of water. Why is he always so mad at me?" I deliberated the reaction to such unintentional accidents.

I'm thankful my father loved me and provided for our

family. It escaped me how most things I did set him off. I never knew what to expect, except the unexpected. He voiced that he loved me at certain periods, but his attitude betrayed those words.

I spent years caught in the wake of his temper flare-ups. As I matured into my teen years, I was rebellious toward him. If he wasn't able to express charity to me, then I was going to throw it back at him.

We had some unpleasant shouting matches in my late teens. I no longer cared to do what he asked. It didn't matter what I did, anyway; it always came back to haunt me.

I can't say I'm proud of the way I acted toward him, but it flowed from my wounded heart. I felt rejected and unimportant. Although I soon forgave him, it would be decades before my emotions caught up.

This unfortunate relationship carried over into my friendship with God. I came to Him at eighteen years old; with a lot of baggage. Good thing God is patient and loving because I needed a whole lot of both patience and love.

YOU MAY BE ABLE TO RELATE.

Do you think God is upset with you or that He wants to beat you over the head for every little mistake? This is a common view of the Lord, unfortunately. If you've struggled with a relationship with your dad, you likely perceive God as indifferent. Unlike fallen people who can't always get it right, God always remains the same.[97] He is trustworthy.

During one of my father's drunken episodes, I jumped out my bedroom window to escape. My mom was always there for my brother and me, but she was regularly preoccupied with distracting my dad from more trouble. I noted black eyes from a few bar incidents. These weren't positive mental photographs that brought security. He never abused me in the physical sense, but he did in his speech.

That old saying about sticks and stones is rubbish. Words have power. They are tools for worthy cause or for ruin. I was so fractured in my heart from his critical, non-accepting verbiage. I developed a lack of self-confidence. When I allowed God in on the heartache, He began a redemptive work in my heart.

The responsibility to treat him kindly was on me. I determined with the grace of God to release him and treat him with respect. It wasn't easy.

One evening after church I arrived home at 8:00 p.m. I tiptoed past the threshold. His disdain toward me permeated the room.

"I don't want you here right now," he articulated from the recliner.

In his defense, I hadn't been a compliant teen. It had finally caught up to me.

My stomach growled. Lunch had been many hours ago. My initial reaction faded under the instruction of the Holy Spirit.

I left. Nourishment for the next several hours came from a box of crackers.

There were months of forced exits when I was instructed to leave. My loving mom was stuck in the middle. I felt for her.

She enlisted several friends to house me when he rejected my presence. Trying conditions. He'd kick me out, then later tell me to come home. This merry-go-round twirled for two years before I finally left for New York. I made concentrated attempts to mend our marred liaison in hopes we would grow closer.

My brother had left for the Air Force Academy, and my mother had started a new job. My allegiance to God was tested. This was where the rubber met the road. I absorbed the brunt of my dad's temper. The pressure was on.

If you or someone you know has felt the sting of rejection, you, too, can find help in the God who stays. Once you surrender to Him, He will never leave you.[98]

HE'S IN IT FOR THE LONG HAUL, THROUGH ALL THE UPS AND DOWNS.

How desperately I needed that solid foundation in my unsettled world.

He is no respecter of persons.[99] He bestows unconditional love and acceptance upon everyone who accepts His Son, Jesus, as their Savior and Lord.[100]

I've no idea what a healthy father-daughter relationship feels like. Yet I've experienced it in the heavenly sense. I've found delight in God as my Father and in His loving care.

A while back, I observed something quite special. I was at a swimming pool, and the glee was clear. A young dad was frolicking in the water with his six-year-old daughter. Up she flew as he tossed her into the wet wonderland. He snuck up on her as she giggled.

She wrapped herself around his back, and they went under together. She squealed with enchantment.

THIS IMAGERY SPOKE TO HOW GOD DESIRES FOR US TO TRUST HIM.

We may sense that the floods of sorrow are drowning us. When storms are swirling around, He longs to be our life jacket in fortifying circumstances and bad ones.

CHAPTER 7

DIRTY DOORS

Door one, two, or three? The question plagued my mind as I contemplated what to do next. Four surgeries had proven ineffective. I'd had a few small parts removed, encountered numerous specialists, and experienced a sea of trial and error. Frustration kept knocking on my threshold. I strove not to answer.

I hadn't learned anything about speaking healing Scriptures over my body or how to stand in faith for my healing. My understanding was more about knowing God, as well as His love for me and others.

I resolved to try the remedy of clipping three nerves. The fact that I would no longer have sexual enjoyment if I were to marry again was irrelevant.

The date for the trip to Los Angeles was set. My mom arrived at my apartment in Texas.

"Why don't you at least get a second opinion?"

I returned to one of the surgeons I had formerly visited but who had never operated on me. We discussed the available options.

"I've had patients who have undergone this procedure you're planning. They aren't any better. Let's reexplore the abdomen through a laparotomy and laparoscopy to be thorough."

"I'm concerned about reopening the scar. I already have scar tissue," I quipped.

"Discuss it with your family, and I'll be back in in a few minutes."

I wasn't ready to unravel, but the storm clouds were taking shape. We mulled over what had been presented.

"I have a cancellation in the morning. A rarity. Here's your bowel prep and surgical papers."

Somewhere in the middle of my drive home, it materialized. I was in the center of a complete meltdown.

Pull over! stunned me out of the mental commotion.

An empty parking lot summoned me. I laid my head on the steering wheel and wept.

"I'm so confused! What should I do? I was all ready to slice the nerves, and now I'm staying here and going a completely different direction?"

The paved area should have posted a warning sign: *Incoming, hot mess.*

"I can't do this anymore! All I want is to be well."

God was wise enough to know I couldn't afford to mull over the assessment, so I sense He made the decision for me. I'm glad He did.

If only I had rested in the promise of Proverbs 3:5–6.[101] The level of entrustment in the Lord grew in phases. Due to my daddy issues, it didn't come to pass straightaway.

The age of thirty-eight emerged. My ability to maintain my career was slipping through my fingers. I had worked in some form from the age of sixteen. The career I'd known since the age of twenty was in threat of converting to a distant memory.

Life can be tricky when we can't see what prowls behind each door.

Seeking God would be an appropriate option. He isn't a celestial fortune-teller who provides a colored trail of candy-coated tell-all. Rather, He longs for us to relate to Him through prayer and listening. The Bible is of utmost importance in discovering His guidance. In it, we find many resolutions to a myriad of issues.

What about those gray areas? There are no specifics stating whether Jim should marry Sally or if Bob should work as an accountant. The keys are found in the Person of God Himself. Frequently, things work out in a step-by-step and a day-by-day process.

If we had the answer to every question, then we wouldn't need God. That would make Him sad. He wants us to draw near to Him, so in the context of relationship, it all works out.

Rolling back the pages of my earlier years in aviation, I remember the excellence our company provided. While I was serving as a flight attendant, it required all hands on deck. The first-class benefits we offered included beverages, appetizers, hot meals, and fudge sundaes. A minute to reach in your pocket and search for keys was a hindrance. Quick access to a cockpit key was necessary. Meal trays in hand, my foot became the tool to prop the door open. Any available body parts were required.

Prepping, serving, and cleanup consumed the air time. One trip reminds me of how I shoved the meal carts in the locked position, took my jumpseat, and *thud*. Harnessing my seat belt before landing didn't even take place in this instance.

Flying has undergone a radical transformation since those days. Doors and locks are more secure.

I moved into a desk job away from the roar of the jet engines."Good morning."

I GREETED A COWORKER ON THE MORNING OF 9/11.

"Our planes were in a terrorist attack," he wailed.

My purse hit the desk, and I joined a large group of employees at our headquarters. In silence, we listened to the reports as they evolved.

I had never tackled the discussions that would ensue that tragic day.

Was Tom's sister on one of the flights? What about the staff member we had relations with in New York? Who had walked through an unsafe accessway on this fateful day?

"Where was God?" shouted devastated souls.

The late Reverend Billy Graham spoke encouraging words to the nation: "No matter how hard we try, words simply cannot express the horror, the shock, and the revulsion we all feel over what took place in this nation on Tuesday morning."

He reminded the country to come together and confess our need for God, and he spoke comfort to people.

He went on to say, "This event reminds us of the brevity and the uncertainty of life. We never know when we, too, will be summoned into eternity. I doubt if those people who got on those planes or who walked into the World Trade Center or the Pentagon on Tuesday thought that it would be the last day of their lives. And that's why each of us must face our own spiritual need and commit ourselves to God and His will."[102]

The weeks following 9/11 shook our land to its core. Our hearts broke for the families and individuals whose lives were forever altered.

A thief had entered the United States and stolen precious lives. Who is the thief described here? The instigator behind the scenes was the enemy.

Solace in such grueling pillage requires muscle not our own.

Jesus is referred to as the Good Shepherd. "I am the door. If anyone enters by Me, he will be saved, and will go in and out and find pasture. The thief does not come except to steal, and to kill, and to destroy. I have come that they may have life, and that they may have it more abundantly. I am the good shepherd. The good shepherd gives His life for the sheep."[103]

The sacred writings occasionally refer to people as sheep. This tender illustration presents the suffering Savior as a caretaker.

Notice this passage says we will go in and out. We have the liberty to live our lives in the safety of One who is there to watch out for and protect us.

Jesus did, in fact, have a choice when He came to the earth. He could have called down thousands of angels and bagged the whole program.[104] He chose to walk through suffering, scourging, beating, and death—for us.

"No one has taken it [My life] away from Me, but I lay it down on My own initiative, I have authority to lay it down, and I have authority to take it up again. This commandment I received from My Father."[105]

He also said He is the door. "Behold, I stand at the door and knock; if anyone hears My voice and opens the door, I will come in to him and will dine with him, and he with Me."[106]

He knocks on our hearts in anticipation we will open up to His forgiveness.

I have known a few friends who manage to discard clutter well. Not everyone is so organized.

Many of us have a dedicated junk drawer. It's the place where unneeded odds and ends go to die. I've even seen an entire room dedicated to such stuff.

The in-laws are due to stay with you shortly. You open the closet. All at once, you're bombarded with debris bursting out at the seams.

There's a phrase relevant to this topic.

"Don't let it take up real estate in your mind."

The challenge to maintain a mental state of clarity is universal. Work, children, and financial struggles can shove their way into our thoughts. They leave little room for anything else.

What about guilt? Or anxiety and stress? They weigh us down like a backpack loaded with rocks.

God wants to bequeath help in the things that preoccupy us.[107]

As God's kids, we can bring all our ugly tendencies and inclinations to Him. He is more than able to handle them, as He already knows about them anyway.

"I FORGIVE. JUST ASK. —GOD," READ THE BILLBOARD ON THE HIGHWAY.

Well put.

The fence to my private world has opened for any who will partake. It's messy, no doubt, but shared to lend encouragement to the injured soul.

Some would say that doors are confining, restricting.

I did a double take. "You've got to be kidding."

Adjacent to me on the freeway was a young man in an old Jeep. Minus the doors.

Traveling 60 mph with the wind slicing through his hair, he didn't skip a beat. Nothing new here.

I prefer the shelter of doors. They can be of tremendous help.

When we travel through life, it's encouraging to know there is somewhere we can go for refuge. The book of Psalms is the perfect place. I love that many of these poetic words echo the cries of our inner man.

How about this one?

"I am weary with my sighing; every night I make my bed swim, I dissolve my couch with my tears."[108]

We can't see the Creator. Liken the situation to a loved one residing in a distant state, who is only a phone call away.

When we belong to Him, God is only a prayer away, and He is always thinking about us.[109]

Two and a half hours later, I was in recovery. The fifth surgical treatment had lasted longer than expected.

The bright lights and sterile environment aroused me into semiconsciousness.

"Dry." I pointed to my mouth.

The nurse popped an ice chip between my teeth.

Soon after, the surgeon showed up bedside.

"You had a femoral hernia. I removed a ligament and placed staples inside your pelvis."

Sounding like a wounded cat, my words were less than legible.

"Another hernia?"

"You also had a nerve that had been trapped in scar tissue from the first hernia repair."

Several weeks passed before I returned to follow up.

"You mean *four* doctors missed a second hernia?"

"Seems so. No exercise for six months."

"Six months!?"

"I'll see you back in my office in a month."

Ouch. Physical exertion divvied up endorphins to assist with the angst. A robust lump of scar tissue nestled its way under the incision.

The calendar pages tumbled to the floor. There was mild improvement. Still, an ever-present clamping sensation dug deep into my digestive tract.

I experienced days of relief on and off for a few years. Most of the affliction recurred. My eventual departure from a long career was inevitable.

Stress at work that trailed the attacks on 9/11 had accumulated to the point of my resignation. I was no longer able to manage the symptoms that wreaked havoc on my health and maintain my position.

The exit was bittersweet. No more trips, benefits, or perks. Although vested, my age had left me with zero monetary compensation. I cherished the special retirement party given by my boss. After seventeen years, I left the great state of Texas.

The sweet spot was that I would later marry my husband of sixteen years. The bonus was my adored stepson.

The first nine years of marriage allotted blessings, yet no health insurance. No more trips to the doctor. A required appointment resulted in paying off the bill over six to twelve months.

I hit rock bottom a year before marrying.

"THIS IS ALL I HAVE LEFT, LORD." I CROUCHED TO MY KNEES WITH FOUR PENNIES AND A NICKEL IN MY PALM.

"I give You my nine cents and a broken heart. Will You please make something beautiful from this mess?"

I stayed with my mom for a while. She helped me through.

"How much is the pay?" I posed the question to the employer.

"Minimum wage."

"When can I start?" I snapped up the first available job opening.

A $9.00-an-hour pay cut would have to suffice. No

room to complain. My career was now in my rearview mirror. The voyages of the past faded away like a pair of worn-out jeans.

I appointed a meeting with myself. The result? Make lemonade. When life hands you lemons, make a tasty drink for someone else. I felt betrayed by my own body, so I dove deep into diet and fitness on an ever-greater level.

I added "certified nutritionist" and "physical trainer" to my list of credentials. I poured my mind into learning anatomy and gaining a weightier understanding of the human physique. I loved imparting wisdom and help to interested females.

God brought me several beautiful ladies ranging from age sixty to eighty. I worked with conditions such as COPD, multiple sclerosis, and Parkinson's. It was sheer gratification.

My work brought me utter satisfaction. The transformation process of seeing another person make positive lifestyle amendments launched exhilaration.

I missed appointments at various times due to debilitating pain. I put forth strong effort for six years into this body of work.

Church and giving were of utmost priority. I was diligent in tithing and attended services as steadily as I was able. Any time there was a prayer for healing, I went forward or raised my hand. As the months and years ticked by, I sought help in spiritual answers for wellness.

"Hi, neighbor," I greeted her as she walked her dogs.

"I don't know if you're interested, but I found something that might be of help to you."

"What is it?" My curiosity was piqued.

"It's a doctor on the East Coast who works with nerve conditions." She delivered the papers to my hand.

"Thank you so much. I'll look into this."

A long stretch went by after the exchange. My husband and I were scheduled to go to California to visit my father-in-law. Enough research revealed a similar professional on the West Coast. The appointment was set.

My gal-pal phoned.

"Your Jeep drove away. We have your money."

"Thank you. You're such a dear friend."

My friend's corner driveway had marked the perfect spot for the sale.

Another sacrifice. No insurance for the very expensive test.

Anguish has a way of projecting us forward to get to the root cause. I had fierce grit to get to the bottom of it.

The costly test was at a facility two hours away. It would be read by the neurosurgeon upon completion.

So many concerns swirling in my head.

"I hope this was the right selection, Lord."

I had prayed and asked for direction more than plenty. Once in California, we would discuss the results of the test.

THE TWENTY-SEVEN-YEAR AWAITED DIAGNOSIS CAME. CERTAINLY NOT WITHOUT COST.

While it wasn't a great report, the mystery was solved. The discovery was a condition named pudendal neuralgia, and I had other damaged nerves as well. My tailbone was also fractured. The money and time was well spent. God had given me an opportunity and made it work together for my good.[110]

Coming up with the hefty amount of money was out of the question. The proposed course of action had an outrageous pricetag. All the out-of-pocket expenses had contributed to bankruptcy and debt. More importantly, the risks didn't thrill me. I had been advised to avoid any more procedures. It seemed they only compounded the problem.

"What now?"

Fasting, soft food, and liquid diets became prevalent.

The first time I ingested spoons of baby food I came to a conclusion. Without a supernatural miracle, I might never enjoy foodstuff again on a regular basis. Humility grew leaps and bounds.

Another colonoscopy.

"Oh, joy."

The images showed a torturous colon. That stands for "twisted." Whether this contributed to my misery and discomfort was up for debate.

Gaining sustenance from nutrition is vital. The exasperation of symptoms from ingesting sustenance incited an atrocious response. I spilled my guts to a physician who recommended an option for relief: enemas.

"Excuse me? Yuck!"

This peculiar protocol was alien.

"Gross, but okay, then."

I was a guinea pig for anything that might work.

The embarrassing routine permeated my nights and contributed to bedtime dread.

Once was not enough. It required two or three each twilight. If the technique wasn't used, it might as well have been like a crab had taken up residence in my gut. Anything that collected manufactured a pinched-off phenomenon that shot flaming needles throughout the affected spot.

"Mercy sakes alive."

I added to my arsenal a TENS unit.[111]

The bright digital numbers weren't favorable: 1:00 to 3:00 a.m. signaled the usual time when my body finally gave in to slumber.

I awoke to the cord of my TENS unit wrapped around my waist and soggy ice packs lining the sheets.

Perseverance gained momentum. I pushed through the displeasure. The complexity of the issues was depleting.

"Can somebody please tell me why it feels like a fiery noose is strangling off my innards?"

"I don't know," came the reply.

A handful of thoughtful medical professionals paused long enough to respond. They couldn't help.

It was as if someone had gone inside and stitched a part of my insides off. When a garden hose gets a gnarly kink, nothing gets through. After a while, it looks like it could explode. The parallel is akin to the displeasure I endured.

Privacy is paramount. When we open ourselves up to reveal our scars and secrets, it makes us vulnerable. Each poke and prod of my body moved me into less concern for the clandestine.

Still, it seems a risk to bare these details.

"Will I be made fun of?"

A few years ago, the matter arose in counseling.

"Do you think I'm going to burst into flames if you tell me?"

The comment made it easier to divulge the hush-hush I held inside.

This remediation brought some sort of natural assistance. The malady resembled a feeling of complete restriction. Shoving a boatload of drugs down my throat didn't bestow the help I sought. I refused to be a pill receptacle.

Inch by inch, my education in natural therapies grew. I migrated toward nontraditional remedies. The list grew. I incorporated fiber, probiotics, aloe vera, slippery elm, and much water. I then added licorice root, magnesium, and alternative therapies, to name a few.

The sanity of my only relief assaulted my nights. My sentiments toward the method was disgust. How could it have evolved to something so grotesque?

I worked with the medical field, ingesting various smorgasbords of new medications. I also voiced my disdain.

"I feel crummy," I replied when inquired of the effects

of any new pharmacon.

Prayer lines and altar calls for healing spurted forth. I began to hear of how Christ not only died for my sins, but also for my health and well-being.

Managing harassing anguish mimicked a full-time job. The quest to learn of spiritual truths for physical ailments vied for my attention. The debilitating enigma inside drove me to desperation. My reliance upon God burst a waterfall of deep dialogue with my Creator.

The concealed mystery woven throughout my loins pushed me to my knees. Again and again.

I stacked the load of men's pants as high as I could and headed for the stockroom. Drops of sweat dripped down my neck and lower back and soiled my shirt.

"Surely everyone will notice I'm soaked," I muttered as I charged to the restroom.

The bundle of paper towels didn't suffice. My face was as red as a cherry tomato.

I had slid into my late forties and early fifties with a bang. I hit menopause to the max.

Hormones are tricky. Although I agreed to spend the money each year for testing and therapy, it was lost in manifestation.

The minutes lost in the restroom added up. If sweat

wasn't excreting like a faucet, my bladder was yelling at me. The medication for bladder control produced an extra plenty of perspiration. Pressure from pelvic pain was more the culprit, so drugs didn't resolve the encumbrance.

I returned to the pants. Crouched down in the corner, it came on like a tidal wave. I was oozing diaphoresis.

This latest ordeal grew in intensity despite the dollars invested in aid. I wasn't able to work more than fifteen minutes without a spigot gushing fluids or having to relieve the pressure on my bladder.

I finally conceded to file for disability. Cancelled sessions and unproductive workdays increased. Friends and coworkers gave numerous comments regarding the suggestion to apply. I smashed into vocational failure.

I threw myself on the bed and bellowed.

"Does God love me? Where did that vibrant young woman go?"

Posterior to these hardships, I knew never to ask that question again.

"Yes. Emphatically. He loves me."

I never imagined this would be my course. I kept believing and praying for different. I didn't welcome the idea but went forward with the filing.

The process was demoralizing. Four years of endless

appeals and denials led to an appearance before a judge.

I was growing in faith for spiritual antidotes but was still engaged in medicinal assistance.

The mailbox delivered the verdict after months. Denied.

All expectation of remediation crumbled.

The daggers dug deep into my wounded pelvis and lit up my entire nervous system similar to a Christmas tree loaded with lights. Like a ragdoll clenched between the teeth of a pitbull, my body was thrashing, seemingly without end.

I've watched the sun set and rise again without a smidgeon of slumber. The following evening replayed incidents as if in a time warp. Two consecutive days without sleep messed with my mind. Harsh scraping like sandpaper stung my eyes. The sanity of function disintegrated with each passing alert nightfall. The compilation of thirty years that contained repetitive lost restoration wore on the psyche.

Others have walked the same road. I empathize.

I'm grateful the cycle of extensive wakefulness hasn't been common; however perpetual, restless, wee hours' alertness has inundated the past three decades.

Thankfully, God holds the capacity to embrace our burdens. I've been chewed up and spit out in an effort to extract benefits for assistance. Never mind that I did have a career once and had worked for those benefits. It was a suitable lesson in futility. If only they knew the torture I've stomached. Literally.

All I wanted to do was give up.

"I'm done! I'm so over this constant combat. My rope is so fried and frazzled. I'm finished."

FRIGID WINTER TEMPERATURES ATTEMPTED TO PRESCRIBE A CHILLY TRAIL ON MY MENTALITY. THE ICY PAVERS LAID A FRAUDULENT PASSAGEWAY.

Relinquish hope. It's no use, resounded from the antagonist.

I followed the faux, nippy thermostat outdoors and looked up. Constellations twinkled above.

"Lord, I don't know what to do. I'm running out of options. I'm impaired and discouraged."

A puffy set of wings drew near. The spotted snow owl flapped by almost cheek-to-cheek. The gorgeous black dots whisked past my hair.

This was no coincidence. The rare sighting befell on the heels of my petition.

I clutched on to Him for dear life. The One who formed my parts in secret negated to let me resign my purpose.

My cries reached His ears. He refused to let me throw in the towel. When I was through, He was just getting started.

In retrospect, I'm glad the filing didn't pan out. God had better for me. A greater resolve to fiercely contest for wellness surged through my veins.

DESOLATION MET DOGMATIC DETERMINATION, AND I SET SAIL TOWARD THE WINDS OF DETERMINATION IN HIS PROMISES.

There is an enemy of our soul. He laughs at our calamity and waits in eager anticipation for us to fold. If we collapse, our destiny will not be achieved. How he works actively to destroy our future.

Are the riptides intimidating you and making threats to pull you under? Know that your life counts. More importantly, it matters to God. It may not seem so at the moment, but there's a testimony in you just waiting to be revealed.

I fasted and sought God's counsel about what door to go through next. The years of endless paperwork put into the potential, yet meager $800 a month were flushed down the drain.

CHAPTER 8
DIRTY DESERTS

Barren. Dry. Dusty. Cactus and tumbleweeds garnish this lonely terrain. Not a plush haven.

Amazing things go on in this waterless land.

Sunshine is a beautiful attribute of the parched plot, and loads of it.

Beautiful rock formations adorn the landscape in many deserts.

What about the glorious dunes that form? These interesting formations can sing. Yes, I did say *sing*.

Climbing or sliding down a dune can cause an avalanche that triggers a 100-decibel "singing" sound caused by a feedback loop of collisions.[112]

Are you in an arid and difficult place?

This was true of my father. In spite of the misfortune in

our kinship, I'm conscious of the skeletons that prowled inside his heart.

Generations pass positive and negative matters to their offspring. Years of tumult between my grandpa and his boy cemented the way for his behavior toward me.

"Gather your belongings. We're leaving." My grandma came to the school for her son.

"Again?" replied her ten-year-old.

Six or more moves and school trades per year were normal. No notice. No warning.

A small, skinny kid, he was bullied. He lacked the ability to form lasting friendships and took on a tough façade to mask his woes. His lack of confidence, combined with great instability, created a myriad of problems. Those troubles cascaded throughout his entire adult life.

The era of the 1940s through the 1960s dealt with mental illnesses in a much more primeval manner. Today we are more educated about what to do. I'm certain he was extremely damaged in his psyche from a lack of love and acceptance from his father. No marvel he wasn't able to award that to me. At seventeen, he began his naval and his drinking careers.

He tried a few rehab programs with exceptional failure. Added to this were many supposed last drunks. Getting plastered into oblivion for the final time never panned out.

I'm still inclined to wish it had been different. It's not okay that he mistreated us and reverberated harsh and disapproving words. Yet the understanding of his lack of parental skills does soften the blow.

The Sustainer of life can deliver refreshment to our weary souls. Like streams in a desert, we are provided help in the Person of Christ.[113]

HEAVEN IS THE HOPE OF ETERNITY WITHOUT TEARS, PAIN, OR SUFFERING.[114]

When we turn our lives over to the Lord, there is the promise of an ever after.

Strong expectation met with disastrous defeat is a recipe for shriveled expectation. The toxins of the enemy's fibs seek to bombard our minds into deeming we aren't worth much.

Have you ever felt like the smallest thing could cause you to explode into shards of flying shrapnel? What about fetching your pillow and pulverizing it into extinction? Feels good, right?

Taking the best and worst of our emotional anguish to a loving Father is acceptable. He doesn't expect us to shellac our grubby thoughts in false pretense. His holiness has seen that the punishment for our marred imperfections was nailed to the cross of Christ.

I've plummeted into some deep caverns. Wandering through the desert will dehydrate your spirit if you don't feed it with God's Word. I had racked up decades of stuffing my face into His book. Without it, I don't know how I would have survived.

One sleep-depleted nightfall, I found myself in a pile of gravel. Dismantled between my endless bathroom trips and traumatized nerves, I crashed. I staggered outside in the dead of night.

"What am I doing out here?"

The dark, starless sky hovered above in silence.

Caught in a vortex of accumulated searing shockwaves and insomnia, I plopped smack into the earth. My red eyes and wrinkled pajamas met with the tears streaming down my epidermis. Not a pretty sight, nor one of my finest moments.

IT'S RAW AND REAL TO BE TRANSPARENT.

Are you knee-deep in muck at this moment? Do you wonder if anyone hears you?

It's 5:30 p.m., and you haven't yet dressed. You watched the hours tick by on the clock as the day ebbed away. Your hygienic tasks disintegrated. Soon the sun will disappear beyond the horizon.

Is there a gnawing anger that rages inside you? You

want to shake your fist at heaven and ask why.

God sees you, my friend, and He knows your name. He knows the number of hairs on your head and beckons you to call out to Him.[115] He longs to fortify your demolished state. This comes about through a relationship with His Son, Jesus.

I experienced unproductive soil in my suffering more times than I preferred. At times, I even felt abandoned and wondered if my situation would ever improve. All my efforts to do everything God's way seemed to fall flat. I knew His promises were true. I knew He couldn't lie.[116] I comprehended that He loved me or He wouldn't have sent Jesus to die for me. But it wasn't working in my life to convert the situation.

It had brought about definite conversion in my character. But was it going to propel me into anything more?

The nagging, ugly voice that challenged my confidence struck with unmerciful blows. Some of the comments were problematic to ward off.

"Why do you keep believing when you've suffered for so long?"

"Why aren't you healed yet?"

"Who do you think you can reach? You're a failure with a dysfunctional body."

"Do you seriously think anyone's going to believe positive things about God?"

I know the drill. The slimy snake fires its evil darts. Its aim is to derail me from moving forward. The enemy has left his stench and slithers off. The trash heap of rubble has to be cleansed with God's truth about me.

The trouble with a falsehood is that it isn't always easy to detect. It can be so subtle that we don't even recognize what's taking place.

The cross is critical for recognition of the love of God. If the blazing winds of life have left you burnt, gaze at the cross. His arms outstretched wide repel any question of how He feels about you.

The ocean waves thunder into the rocks again and again. Their wild sprays leap into the air and crash back again. They sculpt a groove in gradual procession. Before long, the liquid fluid has managed to carve a pattern in the solid substance.

Thought processes and patterns don't mold in an instant. They form in stages and become belief. Oodles of things we perceive about ourselves aren't true.

God doesn't make junk, and He made each one of us. Every human life has value and importance. That worth isn't based on anything we do, have, or possess.[117] Rather, the foundation is solid since we're made in the image of perfection with eternity in mind.

I climbed endless dunes of sand to discover another formation ahead. In the eerie desert, I fought the thoughts that shouted out my demise and utter failure. Would others glean comfort by me sharing my story? Am I able to grant something of substance to confer relief to the hurting? Or do I choose to keep it to myself and remain anonymous?

Despite the pounding heat and elements against me, I pushed on. It's worth the struggle to imagine someone could receive truth and encouragement.

I do not and will not ever say I have all the answers. God alone holds that title. All I know is how to point others to the One who does, even when it seems quiet and He is a million miles away. Don't give up. Keep seeking, keep praying, and keep asking.[118]

Powerful lessons can be accomplished in anonymity. Like humility. It would be nice if character formed when everything around us is fresh, easy, and effortless. There's something about trials that effect conversion.

Christ came to the earth to take on skin and bones. He embodied humility.[119]

It would be unwise to think that as His followers, we could skip the self-effacement.

If Jesus hadn't chastened Himself, there wouldn't have been a way to reconcile mankind to God.

The definition of *humility* is "freedom from pride or

arrogance: the quality or state of being humble."[120]

The blood we bleed is red. It's universal.

If only we cultivated this concept on a more personal level. People are much more likely to be considerate to one another if they are humble. Humility affords us the chance to think of someone beside ourselves. To recognize that we are all alike and no one is better than the other is of utmost importance.

An amazing process transpired in my prayer life. The boldness to pray for anyone and everyone who would allow it consumed my thoughts. Each new prospect fostered excitement. I began praying for women in bathrooms and locker rooms. I welcomed the opportunities to pray in grocery stores, shopping malls, parking lots, and gas stations.

The passionate drive to see someone else set free overtook my actuality. While there remained no improvement for myself, all I thought about was helping someone else.[121]

The wilderness experiences in our lives bring growth. Life springs forth from these obscure places if we allow it.

Out of my desert experience, I developed a deep prayer life. I'm what you would call an intercessor. An intercessor is someone who goes to God and prays for people with needs. They ask for relief and a solution on behalf of the other person.

Knees drawn up in a fetal position is where this petition place ripened.

IT'S HERE THAT I'VE PRAYED FOR INDIVIDUALS ALL AROUND THE WORLD, THOSE WHOSE NAMES I MAY NEVER KNOW—UNTIL HEAVEN, THAT IS.

I relished using the ailment that laid me out on the bed for a higher purpose.

I may have appealed to heaven for you and didn't even know it. God places situations and people on my heart. I go to battle for them in the spiritual realm. I'm thankful that out of a withered and thirsty land, something of beauty has grown.

Adopted as a baby at six and a half weeks, my husband found his home in Los Angeles. As he matured, his perspective on life became muddied. He entered into a desiccated lifestyle at a very early age. His heavy involvement with drugs led him to become a dealer.

Hard partying and reckless living was his norm. On his way to a drug deal at the age of nineteen, he was passed by a vehicle to the left of his Z650 motorcycle. The blunt force knocked him clean off the bike at the acceleration of 60 mph.

For sixty-one yards of highway, he tumbled and somersaulted. The 90-degree temperature blazed. Flesh met pavement, tearing away at his skin. He incurred first-, second-, and third-degree burns on his arms.

He awoke at the hospital minus a spleen. The accident caused a rupture requiring removal.

An interesting combination. A Baptist preacher and a drug dealer. God has a sense of humor.

Four days passed, and the young rebel was able to inch his way to the shower. Hunched over from eighteen stomach staples, he savored the warm water.

He dried himself. The fresh scabs washed away and left rare integument.

He moved at a snail's pace back to bed, cursing up a storm.

He awoke, groggy from a nap. Snapshots of rolling across the asphalt repeated as a video on replay.

"How does your skin feel?" came the voice across the way.

"It burns like *bleep, bleep*!"

The pastor countered, "Imagine what hell would be like—only the burning never stops."

The next few hours entailed in-depth discussion, and a

copy of the Bible passed between the two beds.

Convinced of the Gospel, the young man gave his heart to the Lord.

Not much differed for five years until he got serious about the commitment. He established the need for lasting conversion. Hungry for the Word of God, he repented of his ways.

The addictive lifestyle that had ruled him was over. He was free. He views with remorse the wasted years of drug abuse. Cocaine, acid, mushrooms, opium, nitrous oxide, and alcohol had strangled his soul. Extreme amounts of marijuana were swept away.

The years spent in the desert of destruction still causes him sadness. At present, he is thirty-three years sober. He wishes he had pursued honorable endeavors. The vices in his history hold no enticement to him whatsoever.

He determined to learn the Word of God and serve Jesus as Lord. It was beyond a simple prayer and plans of an eternal benefit package.

What a story of God's love and forgiveness.

"I used to pass the dope, now I pass the hope," he declares. Now an ordained minister, he appreciates the chance to preach in numerous capacities.

It's never too late with God unless you've stopped

breathing. He is as close as your next breath. If you need help or want His Presence, He is there for the asking. But it does call for a shift in direction.

The temptation to fall back into old habits clashes with the anticipation of the new. Reliance upon the power of the Holy Spirit is critical to strengthen our tenacity. Support and recovery groups are also enriching tools.

The beauty of God's grace is that He doesn't want or expect us to clean up our act first. He desires we come as we are and allow His love to come alongside and usher us to a better place.

I MARVEL AT HOW FAR GOD CAN BRING PEOPLE INTO WHOLENESS.

As I look back on our wedding day, I see the exquisiteness of God's redemptive nature.

Cheers and applause erupted throughout the sanctuary. We had waited thirteen months to share our first kiss. Decorated with mercy and grace, I will always treasure that moment of purity. What glory God is able to bring from a mucky past.

CHAPTER 9
THE DIRT ON DENOMINATIONAL DIFFERENCES

Protestant, Methodist, Baptist, Episcopalian, Pentecostal, Catholic: The list goes on and on. How did we get here? There are approximately thirty-three thousand different denominations.[122] The duty of determining what church to attend can be a dizzying task.

Jesus made faith simple enough for a child to understand. How did it get so muddied?

Two motorcycles shared our family garage. When I entered my teens, I rode the "sissy bike." A Honda 90. I blazed through the nearby orchard with my friends in tow.

One lovely day, my brother and I ventured out for an afternoon of riding. He presented me the reins. What a pleasant surprise. I complied.

Confident and assured, I went off the beaten path. The

juicy blackberries glistened amongst the afternoon rays.

I snapped out of my desire to fetch a handful of the tasty treats.

"Go right. Go left," came the command from behind.

"What? Make up your mind."

I did neither. I hit the acceleration and plowed smack into the sharp briars. We tumbled to the clay.

The dust blew off as he patted his shorts.

"What were you thinking?"

"I couldn't make up my mind, so I just went straight."

If memory serves me, I don't remember us partaking in any additional dirt bike excursions.

Have you felt the same frustration about church affiliations? The jumbled route can send you in so many different directions.

A diamond reflects countless facets, depending on how the light hits it.

The church body is comprised of many individuals with varying aspects to it. Repeatedly those peering in from the outside see only malfunction.

Wherein lies the problem?

Although people have a relationship with God through

Jesus, they still possess different personalities and gifts. One person may interpret a passage of doctrine different from how another perceives it.

The result? Scores of denominations. Too many.

With sixty-six books consisting of the Old and New Testament, we are bound to have multiple altered opinions. Some Scriptures are black and white. Then there are those passages that leave readers with an array of interpretations. Regardless, the Word of God is infallible and unalterable. Whether we agree or understand it entirely, it deserves our full attention and compliance.

The Church is chock-full of persons seeking God. It is comprised of those who are new to faith, as well as those who have been in relationship with their Creator for an extended epoch.

HUMANS AREN'T PERFECT. GOD IS THE ONLY ONE WHO FILLS THAT ROLE.

An organism with imperfect souls will produce flaws.

The Greek word for "church" is *ekklesia*, which means "a called-out assembly or congregation."[123] It operates in the fashion of an organism.

An *organism* is defined as a form of life composed of mutually interdependent parts that maintain various vital processes.[124] An *organization* is an organized body of people with a particular purpose, especially a business, society, association, etc.[125]

One is pliable and open to life. The other is a fixed set of established routines.

Don't get me wrong, the Church does have parameters. It should also have the freedom to move in God's Spirit as He designs.

Adhering to the Word of God is still critical. Opinions can be inspiring, but they only go so far. Their importance is of high regard by the individual. What matters is what God thinks and says in His Word.

The Church is also a hospital for the hurting. It does fit that bill, as Jesus Himself said He came for the sick. The pious hurled insults at His questionable guests. He flaunted mercy when He ate with tax collectors and sinners.[126]

Our differences are meant to be reason for celebration. Wouldn't it be grand if they were used as tools to help and encourage one another?

How boring it would be if we were all the same. Our proclivities would also be duplicated. It would be beyond puzzling to try to assist one another if we didn't have dissimilar perspectives.

I use my husband and me by way of illustration. He's the dominant type, and I am gentle and compassionate. If you need a repair or a building job completed, ask him. But he is not the one to run to if you need a shoulder to cry on. That would be yours truly.

I have no clue how to install a door. I'm certain any homeowner would regret hiring me for such a task. It goes without saying the Church has many members, yet it is one body.[127]

Hypocrite. A familiar word. It signifies a person whose behavior does not meet the moral standards or match the opinions that they claim to have.[128]

There is a phrase that helps us comprehend this concern: Christians aren't perfect; they're just forgiven. That is spot-on. When we are gravitating to faith in God, it's best to not determine the outcome based on the actions of others. Only God can be trusted 100 percent, as He is perfection.[129]

I convey some theories of those who claim to know God yet aren't demonstrating the attributes they should.

If a person is new to belief, they are in for a lifelong journey. They aren't going to get everything right all the time. Although they have given their life to the Lord, that doesn't ensure his or her vices will disappear at once. We all struggle, some more than others.

God is patient. He doesn't hit us over the head with a two-by-four. He works with us all of our days to grow and transform us into His image.[130]

I've met followers of Christ who were set free in an instant from their habits and hang-ups. I've also viewed others who wrestle for years with a specific issue.

A celebrity's romances and dark secrets are smeared across magazine covers. Faith is similar. The whole world may be watching, but our selections aren't going to always garner faultlessness.

Personality plays a large part in belief, as well. Peter is a great example. An impulsive fisherman, he made his mistakes.[131] Jesus saw who he would become.

I can almost hear the heated discussions between Peter and John. John was the quiet type, all about love.

At the dinner table, Peter inquired of Jesus, "Lord, and what about this man?"[132]

In essence, Jesus replied, "What is that to you?"[133]

Questions and disputes most certainly arose on occasion.

I envision Peter's outspoken nature. Spontaneous. John's persona was more subdued. Though they loved each other, their temperaments likely clashed on occasion.

What about the abrasive persona? We've all met one or two. They exude the warmth of a porcupine. Say the wrong thing, and you get poked.

An outsider may come to the conclusion that such a one

is not a Christian. We'd hail the notion that their rough edges are still under construction by the Spirit of God.

If you are seeking to know God, it's best to allow Him to reveal Himself to you through the Bible and prayer. It would be fantastic if Christians always represented God in a proper manner.

This acronym gives great insight to the dilemma: PBPWMGINFWMY. It signifies: *Please be patient with me, God is not finished with me yet.*

As a society, we make room for the errors of professionals in their vocations. It's inevitable. Why is it that in the arena of devotion to God, it's not allowed? No grace from others in falling down in our development process. If exactness were a rule to live as a Christian, then what prospect would that allocate to a seeker?

Where does the concept of right and wrong originate?

WITHOUT MORAL ABSOLUTES, SOCIETY HAS NO BOUNDARIES.

The ugly reality is this: Who, then, is the final say?

The moral compass one individual possesses would betray that of another.

One person will have strong judgments on treating others with dignity and respect. The actions of a mistreated person would be the opposite. Their thought processes surround defending and protecting themselves from further insult regardless of how others are affected.

What if the one who was abused attests it is now valid to beat up an individual because they offended him or her? Is it then okay? This paves a slippery slope.

The hard truth is, there must be an original design from which to derive a sense of societal constraints.

This segues into the institution meant to provide a path of direction for mankind. The determination of settling on a denomination presents a challenge. How do you decide? Of necessity is sound doctrine derived from the Scriptures. The Old and New Testaments were designed to be taken as a whole, not as a buffet of picking and choosing.

It's imperative that belief in Jesus' death, burial, and resurrection is taught. Without the resurrection, the Christian faith is meaningless.[134]

Jesus had to be resurrected from the dead or He isn't God. Scripture attests that He rose from the dead and ascended to heaven.[135] After He died, they buried Him in a tomb and sealed it with an enormous stone. The Pharisees saw to it the grave was secure, for fear that someone would take His body and claim He was alive. They had overheard that He'd said He would rise from the dead in three days, and they wanted to ensure no foul play took place.[136]

Can you trust this account? That's for you to decide.

None of us were there. We have to rely on the authenticity of Scripture. I don't know of any other person in the history of mankind who made the claims Jesus did.

Easter is the celebration of Jesus' victory over sin and death. He paid for our eternal security so we would never have to experience separation from the Father.[137] His resurgence from the grave was critical. He would be nothing more than another historical figure without it.

In Italy rests a forty-foot linen cloth deemed the Shroud of Turin. It is believed by many to be the wrapping that covered the body of Jesus in the tomb. There are scholars who support the theory.[138] It goes without saying there are plenty who seek to diminish its authenticity, as well.

From this fabric emanated a fascinating video that depicts how the body of Christ was transformed into a 3D-image statue.

Giulio Fanti is a professor of mechanical and thermal measurements. He is a scholar of the Shroud and led this work for twenty years with his research team.[139] From their analysis, they believe that He received a total of at least six hundred blows. Take some deliberate minutes to process the thought. It's astounding to contemplate the torment He took upon His body for our deliverance.[140]

GRACE. I LOVE THE WORD. UNMERITED FAVOR.

Grace matters when it comes to understanding who God is and with what congregation to align. So often there is a misconception that He is an angry Being, anticipating to take us out. This is a deception and an untruth. God loves people, and He cares about us.

The hardship in the world goes back to the Garden. The forbidden fruit. We are all suffering the consequences of that fatal choice made by Adam and Eve.

God is a God of grace and mercy.[141] *Mercy* is another beautiful word. It has to do with not getting what we deserve. When a child disobeys their parent, they receive discipline or a loss of privileges. We lost our benefits to living in an impeccable world with precise bodies. God put in place a redemption plan in the form of Jesus' atonement.

I've discovered God shows up in some of the most unexpected places. He isn't afraid to tackle the hardest of soil and the stinkiest of situations.

The Church should be a place where we go to know God in a deeper way and receive His love through other believers. Things get skewed when we get off course or lose our focus on Him.

There will never be a spot-on place of worship this side of heaven. Longsuffering is much-needed in associating with our varying differences.

The hot breeze wafted through the air with the putrid odor from the sewer plant. No matter. The party inside the walls far outweighed the offensive scent. The celebration for Jesus was on. The African American church had been home for four years. It was one of my most cherished.

Polished windows aren't required to invoke the presence of God. Some of the most obscure and humble locations have served for great moves of God's Spirit. The distasteful odor never interrupted the amazing blessings our members experienced, peculiar site as it was.

An introduction to the belief for miracles gave birth inside me.

"Watch your words," echoed from the pulpit.

"Speak the Word of God, not your circumstances."

The verbiage splashed across my face like a cold drink on a blistery day.

Resembling a stranger in a foreign land, I was on a mission to learn this new language.

The storm raged on. On the one hand, I was beginning to speak out the opposite of what I felt, yet on the other hand, my symptoms gained ground.

A few part-time jobs, combined with a fitness business, scratched away my energy.

As the sun set behind the clouds, I shed my black slacks

and slipped into comfy night pants. The sparkle in my eyes was swallowed up in the dark circles beneath.

Years of stress had ensnared my body chemistry into a frenetic aberration. Blood tests revealed hormonal dysfunction. Night turned into day and day into night.

"Speak life. Speak life." I combatted the urge to confirm the obvious.

My system shrieked, *Warning, warning, overload.*

At 2:00 a.m., I threw the covers back for the fourth time. Amidst the dark shadows of the room, I tripped over a foreign object. My forehead smacked into the bathroom door.

"Alright then!" My speech sprang into action:

"Oh, give thanks to the Lord for He is good. For His mercy endures forever."[142]

"By His stripes I was healed."[143]

The next day, I began again. I spoke scriptures of healing out loud in defiance of the raging inferno inside and went to work.

Fire is a purifier and a destructive force.

The biblical text refers to our trials as "fiery."[144]

No one welcomes trouble. Jesus comes alongside and empowers us if we allow it. Misfortune makes us stronger and more resilient after it subsides. The Holy Spirit empowers our inner man to endure hardship.[145] We can then be used to encourage others who are going through tough seasons.

A rural district very close to where we reside was enveloped in flames in an instant. The late-night hours exploded into a frenzy.

High winds broke a tree that fell on a power line. A spark ignited an inferno that plowed through an entire community. Hundreds of homes became a war zone within two short hours.

Many of these people were homeowners or acquaintances. We'd shared laughter and meals. One moment all was well, and within minutes nothing was the same.

The once-lush forest of foliage was now a smoldering ruin of ash and smoke.

It's impossible to find the words for such sadness. The outpouring of all the donations was exquisite. Hugs and tears lingered for weeks. These acts of charity are the representation of what Christ asks of us.

Natural disasters run amok. When catastrophe strikes, we can be the hands and feet of Jesus to those who are in distress. This is how the Church should operate in turbulence.

CHAPTER 10
THE REAL DIRT ON DEATH

Death. Serious stuff. One out of one of us dies. Staggering odds. We should assign vigilant deliberation to where we will spend eternity.

It's a troublesome fact. We all have an expiration date.

It's distressing to lose someone we love or a beloved pet. The afterlife illuminates our thoughts. Is there such a thing? Do we stop existing after death? Does a part of us go somewhere else when we die?

Facing mortality is morbid. We do our best to ward off this enemy through many methods. Eating well and exercising can prolong our lives and slow the aging process. The end is still inevitable.

Materials are available to prepare for death in the way of wills, living trusts, and prearranged funerals. Though helpful, they do not contribute to ensuring where we go when our bodies return to the earth.

I was twenty-six when my fifty-two-year-old father passed. It was a tragic end to a sad life. Oodles of unfinished business loomed in our liaison.

Like it or not, I had to face the facts. My dad was gone. He would never be there to work on what could have been more mending for our tumultuous affinity.

I enjoyed a trifle of cheery moments with him when I moved out. I had my own life and resided in Texas. He was a bit better toward me. Still, our relationship was cut too short.

A week before his passing, he initiated talks with God. He also began to read his Bible again. I take comfort in these actions. It's my hope he had come to discern the need to release his own father of offenses, as well.

Our last encounter wasn't much different than our previous history. I sat next to his emaciated body and massaged his hand. He grew tired from the left-sided paralysis.

I couldn't fathom that we would get in an argument. We had been engaged in a positive situation. I don't even remember what brought it about.

His attitude was somewhat hostile, so I proceeded to the bedroom to pray. I perched my hands on the windowsill and asked God for assistance.

"Please help me be kind," I pleaded.

After several minutes, I resumed our meeting and made amends.

That fateful day marked the last moment I saw him.

How frequently do we take for granted there will be more time? Will there be another possibility to say "I love you," or "I'm sorry"?

I thank God for the fortitude with which He equipped me. I shudder to ruminate the remorse I would have experienced had I not taken the high road. Years of practice prepared the way.

Many around the globe have had to deal with the demise of someone so dear whose life was cut short. Grief brings hopelessness. It is a road none of us wishes to take.

Heaven is the hope of that which is permanent.

The "ever after" is of great debate to some.

It was not my intention to unmask scrupulous areas of my private anguish. Yet, as God's Spirit leads, it's important to rectify a reality. Unspeakable components have woven together the tapestry of my story.

Heaps of trepidation precede the unwrapping of my dad's passing. Few are aware of the bitter facts. I recoiled when questioned. The wretchedness of giving thought to the instance was overpowering. I responded that he had experienced a heart attack and a stroke. True enough.

Those two conditions led to his demise but didn't embody the final chapter.

A 95-pound semiparalyzed frame was more than he could bear. He was unable to walk, he peed himself constantly and had lost ninety pounds. He fell off the toilet, landed on the floor, and lost his independence.

Though we did all we could to assist him, and even brought in home health care, it wasn't enough to sustain his dispirited mind. My heart broke in two. My knees wore out from entreating my eternal Father on his behalf.

Many individuals are unsung heroes. My mom is one of them. She juggled a full-time job and spent every other waking moment giving him the best of care. She went above and beyond the call of duty, despite how he treated her. Faithfully she served at my bedside for every surgical procedure, as well.

One unsuspecting day around my twenty-sixth birthday, I received a phone call from my mom. The wreckage that engulfed him had halted. He had taken his own life.

Later we found a couple of choice notes from Dad articulating his love and appreciation for us. Still, we only encountered these so many years after the fact. The departure note, however, was located immediately. At least he exhibited consideration by disclosing the fact that he was sorry.

IN SUCH A CRISIS, ONE SCRATCHES FOR OPTIMISM.

There are myriads who have carried the crucible of torment from a similar occurrence.

An explosive bomb went off inside me at the news. I would never be able to capture what I had tried to extract from our strained relationship.

The continual expectation I always held that we would someday be whole shattered in a million pieces. I had never surrendered the desire to see him set free.

In the months up to his exit, he attempted the impossible. He went to inquire about regaining his previous truck-driving position. My mom recounted the instance to me. Heart-wrenching.

The office was abuzz with work orders and invoices. Truck drivers entered and exited. In walked my dad in his paltry state, assisted by my mom. She facilitated him to the corner office. His insistence wore on her resolve not to pursue the predictable. He was adamant.

"Can I have my job back?"

The rest is overtly clear. His mind couldn't accept what his body knew to be true.

I'm aware there are others who have lived through similar happenings. It's to you I present the antidote that has soothed my wounds.

There is great pleasure living with anticipation. Eternity lies ahead for those who come to Christ and give themselves to Him.

In the beautiful affair of humanity, it's important to know who we are.

People have three parts: spirit, soul, and body.

There is the scientific synopsis of the three, as well as the biblical.

The body is the physical substance of the human organism, composed of living cells and extracellular materials and organized into tissues, organs, and systems. It is explained as biochemical reactions and actions that include the mobilization of hormones, chemicals, neurotransmitters, fluids, and bodily tissue.[146]

The Heart Math Institute has compiled over twenty-five years of scientific research on the psychophysiology of stress, emotions, and the interactions between the heart and brain. The effect of heart activity on brain function has been examined extensively over the past forty years. Different patterns of the heart activity have distinct effects on cognitive and emotional function.[147]

The spirit is linked with the informational, quantum-state level, which is responsible for bodily responses acting upon external, and internal informational interchanges, which adversely affect functioning on a cellular to a systematic level.[148] Science recognizes that we do own three parts.

Now the biblical view.

The body is made up of flesh and bones.

The soul, in biblical terminology, encompasses the mind, the will, and the emotions. This includes our ability to choose. The Greek word for "soul" in the Bible is *psyche*, which is also the root word of *psychology*.[149]

The spirit is the deepest part of our being. God created our spirit man so we could come into relationship with Him.[150]

It's up to you what you do with the presented data and how you will proceed.

Some folks may say, "Nonsense."

They are free to come to that conclusion. It's also a wish that many will ponder the information thoroughly.

Biblical doctrine tells us that God is no respecter of persons.[151] What He makes available, He makes accessible to everyone. No one is excluded, should they respond. Jesus made it possible for us to have the privilege of going to God Himself without a priest. He is now the High Priest to whom we have access.[152]

When we were born, our spirit was intact—but it was dead. What does that mean? We are all born into the family of Adam, and through him, we all inherited a hostile foe. It's entitled: sin.[153]

Sin means "to miss the mark" or "to fall short."[154]

God is holy, perfect, and sustained by Himself. In other words, He doesn't need anything beyond Himself to exist.[155]

The conflict is, how can a holy God and unholy people merge? Can two polar opposites connect?

Without a doubt, there are wonderful, special people in the world. But there needs to be a standard.

Let's say you get up one Saturday afternoon and get a wild hair. You drive to an unfamiliar part of town and select a random house. The owner opens the door.

Without hesitation, you strut by the stranger and plop your bottom on their sofa. Your bravery extends to reaching for the remote as you kick your feet up on the coffee table.

Sound ludicrous?

This bizarre scenario sets an illustrative stage; it mirrors the brashness of telling the Creator of the universe how we're going to relate to Him.

The concept is clear. This rude and abnormal behavior would create a frenzy in the house. Yet do we give thought to recognizing the guidelines God has laid out for us to know Him?

THERE IS A DECEPTION FROM THE ENEMY TO CAUSE US TO CONJURE UP OUR OWN GOD.

He is a liar and an unseen masquerader who assaults our self-worth and association with our Creator. He is hateful and evil to his core. He knows nothing of love, light, or freedom.[156]

The foreboding shadows conceal his objective to seduce us into invisible chains of bondage. He relishes the idea of paralyzing his victims with fear. The goal is to cripple our desire to know God. He sets out traps, hoping we'll fall into a pit and remain. He hates everything about God and what God loves most: people.

What better plan than to fire hell's darts at mortals every way he and his demonic forces can? He is crafty and sly.[157]

Water-skiing was my favorite sport in high school. The large local lake was domicile for summer. My boyfriends' family owned a super-cool boat. We had such a blast.

Once I began my career in the airlines, the good fortune to unwind on a Texas lagoon was seldom. I had a new guy years later who also had a watercraft. We couldn't wait to get to that refreshing spot to overcome the sweltering heat.

One afternoon elucidates. I took a turn in a calm cove and squeaked by a lengthy knotted barbed wire that had wrapped itself around an item. Any closer and it could have been disastrous.

Our opposing foe is much the same. He pounces when least expected and banks on destroying us. There's no red flag waving in the air announcing his coming. He lurks in dark, unsuspecting moments and ambushes just like a lion on injured prey.

Only God can equip us to confront the enemy with courage and fearlessness.

Jesus' ministry didn't start until He had experienced temptation. Imagine the hunger pangs from forty days without food. The devil slithered in for the attack.

Jesus' weapons of offense weren't swords or rocks. His line of defense is the same for us today: the spoken Word of God.

While in the desert forty days and nights, He fasted and became hungry.[158]

Great discipline is summoned to abstain from foods. I'm familiar with it to the degree of how often I've reverted to it for relief from symptoms.

When Jesus was at His weakest, the dark antagonist seized the opening.

The coaxing appeared in the form of physical sustenance.[159] The second assault blasted in with the notion of testing God.[160] The devil went for the jugular in the third round. He offered Jesus pseudo-power.[161]

How repeatedly we give in to the wrong desire when our resistance is down. We have an Advocate who has walked the path before us.

Many scholars give reason for this temptation, explaining why it took place. One resource describes the case as follows:

"So that this account of Jesus' triumph over the attack of Satan will show us Christ's power of his arch enemy, the devil, thus establishing Himself as the true Sovereign King, it will prove that He is stronger than the devil and therefore has the power to rescue sinners from the kingdom of darkness; it will prove that He is sinless and thus has a right to be our Holy Redeemer and it will also show the practical path to triumph in temptation.

"And so I say it's a monumental portion of Scripture."[162]

Scripture refers to Jesus as the last Adam.[163] He was the God-man. His mission was to bring salvation to the world, [164] to live and die as a perfect, sinless sacrifice.[165]

He is qualified to be our High Priest. Because He endured temptation, He sympathizes with our weaknesses.[166]

It's of tremendous value to know that even Jesus wasn't

allocated a shortcut or a quick fix. God saw fit for the Savior of the world to contend with the lure of enticement before providing help to us.

That would be easy if He were on the earth as God and not human. The reality is that He was both. He laid aside His divine privileges to become flesh and bone.[167]

THE COST WAS CALCULATED. THE ANSWER WAS YES.

Still, Jesus toiled over the reality of the cross. He asked the Father if there was any other way.[168] He could have called down legions of angels to rescue Him.[169] But then there would have been no way for us to have reconciliation with the Father.[170]

God always has a good plan for our lives.[171]

Speaking of good, sometimes it's nice to dabble in a bit of sweet treats. My thoughtful spouse blessed me with a lovely delight. The cupcake on the counter smiled back at me.

I'm free of allergens.

"You do look scrumptious. Maybe just a few bites."

I melted into the moment of temporary bliss.

The next day didn't go well. For three years, my complexion had resembled a dot-to-dot design. The slightest deviation of pantry choices displayed little white bumps combined with bright red spots bedazzling my cheeks. Such precious few cooking options and still havoc on my skin or insides.

Not again. Where can I hide?

I stood on the old, weathered deck as the sun set, wardrobed in the same ratty T-shirt from the previous day. The blue sky turned to dusk. Orange tones shimmered on the horizon. I held the broom and inquired of the Lord.

"Will I ever get out of these travail rags? I long to go to the ball."

Once again, moist droplets plunked to the wooden structure beneath my feet.

The images of clothing articles that hung in the closet danced across my mind. New pricetags poked out in assorted locations. Some dated back a few decades. I had stopped wearing makeup and jewelry for quite a stint. Except for when I went to church, dressing up entailed too much energy. Even that was minimal, at best.

It can be difficult to believe God is working out a plan for our best.

Is your back against the wall? How do you contend for better?

When nothing made sense, I told Him, "I know You're real and that You're good."

The language of heaven kicked in.

"Well, hallelujah! In spite of it all. Even if I do have spots."

Positive affirmations bubbled inside me.

"I can expect beneficial things to come from all of this," I declared.

I surmised that the Lord had some reconfiguring to do in me. Every now and then, planes are taken out of service to revamp. The purpose is to accommodate more passengers or to reduce the number of seats. Either way it's for a specific purpose. I'm supposing that my hardships will bring encouragement to anyone who needs it.

Take heart if you've experienced a significant amount of turbulence. Allow Jesus to calm the stormy sea.[172]

Everything God does is counterfeited by the devil in a twisted version. If God wants us to wait for something, He sees the how and why. The evil one wants us to short-circuit God's timing so we will take the comfortable path and subvert the right pathway for us.

How do you spot a counterfeit? Bankers don't study fake money. They become familiar with the authentic.[173]

If we don't know the real deal—God—we can be fooled by the devil into thinking something is best for us when it's not.

Some may be saying this is far-fetched or superstitious. Yet how can you explain much of the evil that takes place if there isn't a wicked force at work? Where else do you attribute it? And if you don't believe in God, then how can you say that it's His fault if He doesn't exist? This is an effort to expose the enemy for the louse he is.

We make mistakes and do things we ought not to do. This causes privation for others. Underneath it all, the disarray of this world began with an opposing force to homo sapiens.

So, who is this foe? What is he about, and what is his motivation? Let's get to the dirt and soot of the truth. We will piece Scriptures together that describe where he originated. The puzzle fits together, revealing his identity.

The first place he comes onto the scene is in the Garden. His nasty manifestation is found in the Gospels. One distinct incident is in the temptation of Christ.[174]

He is described as a serpent.[175] Matthew 8:28–34 and Mark 5:6–13 state that demons can inhabit animals and people. He entered into Judas to betray Jesus.[176] He is a murderer and the father of lies.[177]

Revelation is the last book of the New Testament, and it depicts what will come to pass at the end of the age and of heaven and hell. Daniel and Ezekiel complement Revelation in harmonic symphony. They expound in detail what is still to come.

This is not meant to be a fear tactic to coerce people to approach God out of terror. God does not promote fear. The authority of Scripture tells us that "God has not given us a spirit of fear, but of power, of love and of a sound mind."[178] God is much stronger and more powerful than the devil.

This is definitely one of my least-favorite subjects. It is bound to arouse questions and skepticism.

I'd much prefer to discuss the love and goodness of God than delve into this abysmal topic. But if we're to go deep into the concept of His attributes, then the opposite should be investigated, as well.

Many individuals acknowledge angels. They deem their presence is real. Yet they don't profess belief in God.

THERE IS AN INTRIGUE SURROUNDING THESE CELESTIAL BEINGS.

When we are seduced, it doesn't come from God. He does not tempt anyone and cannot be tempted by evil.[179]

"Hold it a minute," you say, "Jesus was invited to deter from the path of holiness."

Yes, He was, but He also overcame. God is light, and in Him there is no darkness at all.[180]

Check and see if you know of one person who has never done anything wrong. Even if they were pretty close, it's unreasonable to consider that specific one hasn't ever had a bad thought.

Jesus' desert experience on earth was for a specific season and purpose. Once He was resurrected, He no longer resides in the mortal body He possessed on earth, but in a perfect body, now in heaven.[181]

The origin of iniquity derives itself from free will. Angels are also created beings with the option to choose.[182] The book of Genesis speaks of them. Their appearance dates back to the earliest text of the Bible.[183]

In mankind's original state, there wasn't a consciousness contrary to virtue. The only power known to Adam and Eve was love and goodness.

Curiosity. They allowed it to get the best of them. They made the fateful decision to examine the Tree of the Knowledge of Good and Evil. Shame crashed into their souls. Their eyes were opened.[184]

Discontentment and dissatisfaction. Could this have been a scenario in Paradise? The first opening to this deadly duo reared its ugly snout in heaven.

Many scholars surmise that Satan was once a beautiful angel. He held a prominent position in heaven. He decided that wasn't enough. He aspired to become God, having all power, authority, and control.[185]

At first glance, the referenced Scripture seems to

extend toward the king of Tyre. Allegories, parables, and illustrations refer to varied themes. Further probing gives us the ability to comprehend. Theologians have spent years in prayer and study to give us perception.

Greed for power is nothing new. It has played out throughout history.

God is the only One who is wholly perfect and able to use His power for the benefit of others. Deuteronomy 32:4 mentions this: "The Rock! His work is perfect, for all His ways are just; a God of faithfulness and without injustice, righteous and upright is He."

Other names attributed to the devil are "the dragon,"[186] "Lucifer,"[187] the "prince of darkness,"[188] and "the accuser."[189] He is also shown as the thief,[190] the tempter,[191]and the deceiver of the whole world.[192]

The sacred text gives explicit warnings to steer clear of the foul forces.[193] Job records an interaction between Satan and God.[194] The details unveil the assault launched against this man of God. The devil was roaming the earth.[195]

Does this sound like something out of a horror film—demons roaming the earth wreaking havoc and destruction? It fits the bill for any fantasy of dark indulgence. Is this the result of our imagination, or is there any validity to its actuality? Decide for yourself, but isn't it evident we are not living in utopia?

It's important to notice that Jesus is the Prince of Peace. He is the reverse of destruction and disorder.[196]

The book of Isaiah is full of imagery. It was prophesied from 739–681 BC. It also tells of the coming Messiah, Jesus;[197] His virgin birth;[198]and the death He would face for mankind.[199] Isaiah chronicles the devil's fall from grace.

The Bible is a fascinating book. What a great read! Delve into ancient civilizations and their encounters with God, angels, and demons. The prophet Isaiah wrote in poetic depictions and descriptions.

Isaih 14:12 commences the unfolding of what took place in the firmaments.

"How you have fallen from heaven, O star of the morning, son of the dawn! You have been cut down to the earth, you who have weakened the nations!"

"But you said in your heart, 'I will ascend to heaven; I will raise my throne above the stars of God, and I will sit on the mount of assembly in the recesses of the north. I will ascend above the heights of the clouds; I will make myself like the Most High.' Nevertheless you will be brought down to Sheol, to the recesses of the pit."[200]

At first glance, it would seem difficult to relate this precise passage to the enemy. It states he will make himself like the Most High. He wants to be God. No longer was he satisfied to be an angelic creature. He now aspired to be God himself.

God is the only Being that can see and know everything, making Him omniscient: "Remember the former things, those of long ago; I am God, and there is no other; I am God, and there is none like me. I make known the end from the beginning, from ancient times, what is still to come. I say, 'My purpose will stand, and I will do all that I please'."[201]

The unfortunate account of Job's desolation includes a rendering of God's response. Job poses his heartbreaking questions. God responds with an exposé on His creative powers and divine nature.[202]

When the devil was thrown from heaven, he became an enemy of God. He no longer held a position in God's kingdom and has no future with Him. He is an outcast.

THIS CATACLYSMIC FLASH IN THE HEAVENS SPARKED A FEROCIOUS FIRE.

The explosive aftermath would mar and distort mankind for the unforeseeable future. That is, until the Messiah would come.[203]

The prophet Zechariah depicts an act of Satan. It tells of his attitude toward society:

"Then he showed me Joshua the high priest standing before the angel of the Lord, and Satan standing at his right to accuse him."[204]

Notice it says he "accused." This has been his lifelong pursuit: to accuse and assault mankind.

The enemy is not alone in his plight against God and civilization. One-third of the angels of heaven followed him in his rebellion:

"And there was war in heaven, Michael and his angels waging war with the dragon. The dragon and his angels waged war, and they were not strong enough, and there was no longer a place found for them in heaven. And the great dragon was thrown down, the serpent of old who is called the devil and Satan, who deceives the whole world; he was thrown down to the earth, and his angels were thrown down with him."[205]

God stated that all He had made was "very good," so it's certain that his archenemy would be in favor of all that is bad.[206]

Why did Jesus have to come to earth, suffer, and die? What a blockbuster of a movie! Battles of good and evil irradiate the atmosphere. Society sits in the middle of a catastrophic supernatural war.

When my husband was in his early twenties, he took a trip to Israel for six months. He recounted to me a noteworthy sundown when he sat upon the Mount of Olives. He gazed upon the scenery surrounding this historic location. The disciples had frequented this mountain with their Lord.

"Why did Jesus have to go through such torment?" he inquired of God.

He felt that God spoke to him in his heart: *It was the only way.*

I admit that I don't comprehend the concept of sacrifice and shedding of blood for the forgiveness of sins. But in my finite understanding, I can't grasp the mind of God. He is a mystery and beyond comprehension.[207]

He is self-sufficient and all-knowing and needs nothing outside Himself for survival. The beauty of this is that He longs for us to belong to Him. He derives joy and pleasure out of having relationship to His created beings.

Billy Graham made mention that some have named Christianity a "bloody religion," but ignore the atrocities in other world religions.[208] He, too, encountered many who balked at the idea of the shedding of blood for forgiveness. Jesus shed His blood for all of humanity: "Without the shedding of blood there is no remission of sin."[209]

Not one individual has accomplished a faultless life. The perfection of Jesus' life was the only solution. His substitution for our lack of holiness provided the spotless, sinless remediation.[210]

Jesus' death, burial, and resurrection awards us an opportunity. We are invited into eternal fellowship with

God. Christ took on Himself our past and present sins. When we identify with Him in His sacrifice, we become acceptable to God.[211]

I learned the hard way that resisting God's ways doesn't pan out. My stubborn seventeen-year-old self wasn't making wholesome choices. My entanglement in lustful desires brought to light my desperate need for God. Submission was the only option.

God is always willing to allow us to learn for ourselves. He is long-suffering.

A quote from Amy Thomas goes as follows: "I guess it goes to show that you just never know where life will take you. You search for answers. You wonder what it all means. You stumble, and you soar. And, if you're lucky, you make it to Paris for a while."

THANKFULLY, WITH GOD, THERE'S MORE THAN STUMBLING AND MAYBE MAKING IT TO PARIS.

France is rich in food, architecture, and culture. *Oui, oui.*

A trip to Nice, France, was one of my holiday expeditions in the past. My gracious brother took me to see the sights as he was a well-rounded world traveler with the ability to adapt to foreign languages with ease. Yet, with all its grandeur, it's not heaven.

We don't have to go on a treasure hunt for a heavenly locked vault to find Him. He makes a way for us to come to Him on His terms, and He makes it available to all. No one is exempt.

To become a member of God's family, we have to go through Jesus.[212]

The brutality of the beating He endured ripped the epithelium right off His body. While He was tortured, scoffers hurled their insults at Him. They mocked and spit on Him. He uttered no words of retort. He absorbed the injury.[213] Why? For us. If He had chosen to dismiss this critical move in history, there would have been no deliverance. He had each of us in mind when He suffered.

Repent. The word is ageless. However, due to poor descriptions, it has been shunned by many. The original Greek word is *metanoia*.[214] It means "to change your mind."

Herein is the quandary. Where does the power to do so originate? How does one do a 180-degree turn away from sin? Simple. Replacement. Turn *toward* God. Understand that Jesus brought a whole new covenant to us. No longer are we bound by burdensome weights we were never meant to bear. We are to see the Father in the reflection of Christ and recognize the payment for our malfunctions has been made.[215]

When we fall in love with Him and appreciate the price

He paid for us, we realize the heartfelt desire to live in His ways.

God has already taken care of everything we need. Our part is simply to place our faith in the truth that Jesus took on Himself our sins.[216]

The notion that we must get cleaned up before coming to God is impractical and unattainable. We are to come as we are, in recognition of the truth that we don't hold the capability to make ourselves impeccable.

Maybe you've been bruised and battered, and you think all you can do is surrender in bits and pieces. He will take all your splinters and work with you one step at a time.

Arguments ignite tension. Raw emotions and anger spring from conflict. Once the dust has settled, someone has to make amends. Resolution requires one or both parties to apologize.

It's unusual to remediate conflict without using the word "sorry." It's the same concept with repentance. It means admitting to God we have fallen short of His standard.

He is not waiting to laugh at us and say, "I told you so."

God wants us to succeed. Why would He have made the ultimate sacrifice otherwise? When we identify with Jesus in His death on the cross, God sees us as pure and forgiven. But it requires that we ask Jesus into our hearts and yield to His ways.

Shame and fear plague the soul. What a divine exchange it is to release these enemies and receive freedom in Christ.[217] God hates sin because it's not healthy for us and it hurts others.

Selah. The word appears frequently in the book of Psalms. It is understood to convey a pause.[218] The cross of Christ demands a silence.

After an extreme scourging, His hands and feet are hammered through with large nails securing His body to the cross.[219] A horrific incident for any parent. God the Father endured the unimaginable. His overwhelming love for us placed His only Son on that cross to pay our penalty.

The result?

WE CAN NOW ENJOY FREEDOM FROM THE GRIPS OF ALL THAT ATTEMPTS TO SLAY, DESTROY, AND DISGRACE US. IT'S THERE FOR THE ASKING.

Jesus knew the inevitable. He was slain before the foundation of the world.[220] His tender skin would undergo cruel lacerations. Blow by blow, the nerves would send excruciating pain throughout His body.[221] His loving hands bore the agony of the huge nails that pierced Him.

The hate and repugnance launched at Him was for what? Healing the sick, restoring sight to the blind, and raising the dead. It was His pure and unadulterated love for all that commanded such commotion.

A Roman flogging was no laughing matter. *A short whip with several single or braided leather thongs of variable length were weaved together. Small iron balls or sharp pieces of sheep bones were tied at intervals. The man was stripped of clothing and his hands were tied to an upright post. The back, buttocks, and legs were flogged by two soldiers or by one who alternated position.*

As the Roman soldiers repeatedly struck the victim's back with full force, the iron balls would cause deep contusions, and the leather thongs and sheep bones cut into the skin and subcutaneous tissues. As the lashing continued, the lacerations would tear into the underlying skeletal muscles and produce quivering ribbons of bleeding flesh.[222]

The holy Christ experienced sin for the first time. In this pivotal moment in history, He knew the full effect of depravity. The torrential storm of man's hate and shame encompassed His being. Guilt, lies, and abuse wagged their ugly tails at Him. The wickedness of all civilization surged through His physical frame. He hung there, broken for us. He bore our punishment.[223][224] The reason? Love. Pure, unconditional love.

God bequeaths acceptance and forgiveness when we ask Jesus into our hearts, and He provides His righteousness for us.

THE HOSTILE JOURNEY OF THE CROSS WAS THE EPITOME OF GETTING DIRTY.

The crucifixion is portrayed in in Mel Gibson's movie *The Passion of the Christ*. The cinematic production is as close to the brutality of the real thing as I've ever seen.

It's an imperative point to understand that Jesus died, was buried, and rose on the third day.[225] Countless Scriptures record His execution.

Why is this so important? If Jesus hadn't risen from the dead, then He made false claims of being God, He died, and that was that. If He had perished and the story was over, there wouldn't be anything supernatural about it.

Paul L. Maier, professor of ancient history at Western Michigan University, writes that *"Flavius Josephus was a Jewish historian born in Jerusalem four years after the crucifixion of Jesus of Nazareth in the same city. Because of this proximity to Jesus in terms of time and place, his writings have a near-eyewitness quality as they relate to the entire cultural background of the New Testament era."*

Professor Maier continues, *"Josephus referred to Jesus of Nazareth twice. In Antiquities18:63—in the middle of information on Pontius Pilate (A.D. 26–36)—Josephus provides the longest secular reference to Jesus in any first-century source."*[226]

Other historical documents chronicle the life and

execution of Christ.[227]

His resurrection was a display of monumental proportions. This single act conquered the devil, who had aspired to win the war and become God.[228] Because Jesus overcame death, He defeated its very source: the devil and his works. His victory in overcoming the grave is what the entire faith of Christianity hangs on. Otherwise He was only another prophet.

Paul writes of the imperative importance of this occurrence.[229]

When we rest in the finished work of Christ, we experience peace. The Holy Spirit teaches us to hear God's voice.[230] The exhaustive task of relying on our own resolve is over.

I believe my dad was saved. That may surprise many. I'm aware his life was a disaster.

He made a commitment to Jesus when he was young. His family was dirt poor. During the Depression, food was scarce. Proper nourishment eluded him. His inner man was plagued with deep wounds. Alcohol anesthetized his suppressed distress. The awareness he wasn't proposed to live life in God through his own efforts wasn't comprehended.

My father made countless attempts to get his act together, as well as attend church. The established spiral sucked him back into old patterns. If only he had relied upon the power of God's Spirit. The last week of his life is the only consolation I have in reference to his salvation.

He was no longer able to purchase beer for himself. Sobriety at last. Twelve months of abstinence from alcohol had arrived, although it was involuntary.

Sparkles of glitter brighten my thoughts as I've ripened. Impressions of nourishing deliberations sway in my reflective recollections.

I was provided for. A worn, musical teddy bear sits amongst my valuables. A precious jewelry box and a dress I wanted join their chorus. They sing out the golden few blossoms scattered in mercy from my dad.

He accompanied me two hours to one of my first modeling gigs. Despite skipping all my cheerleading events, he showed up at the last minute to see me crowned Homecoming Queen.

Splendor and loveliness sprinkle my adolescence with inhales of few and far between gifts. Praises to my Lord for the blessing to behold the fragile reminiscences that assist my heart to heal.

John chapters fourteen through seventeen are beautiful passages. They provide perceptiveness into the purpose of the Holy Spirit. Jesus spoke loving words to His disciples before the crucifixion. These words can apply to us, too, if we have given Jesus first place in our hearts.

The Holy Spirit is with us always when we belong to God.[231] How wonderful to know we have an Advocate and a Guide.

Factory work is no easy assignment. Accidents occur, revolving around dangerous machinery.

Imagine a serious injury such as an employee losing a limb. The CEO receives word and sends a representative on his behalf.

This individual holds the same authority as the chief executive officer. He handles the incident with the proper resources.

The Holy Spirit is the representative of Jesus. He carries out His work on earth as He receives instruction.

A warm, fuzzy blanket on a cold winter's night provides soothing relief. Compare it to another word that describes the Holy Spirit: *paracletos*. The Greek word means "comforter."

He wants to be there to refresh and renew us when we need reassurance. It would be nice if we could always feel His presence, but He is there—in Spirit.

He will always be available when we call on Him. He never hangs up. The line is always open.

I'm a hugger. For years, I've been notorious for hugging

perfect strangers. I enjoy the sensation of physical touch. It's such a joy to see the expression on a person's face when they don't know me and yet I come toward them in friendliness.

We most likely aren't going to have the experience of the Holy Spirit brushing our bodies like a soft feather. This is why we have one another. We are His essence when we bring interactions that depict His presence.

IF ONLY THERE WERE MORE HUGS IN THE WORLD AND LESS ANIMOSITY.

CHAPTER 11

DIRTY DELAYS

Setbacks. Obstacles. Delays. You gain an inch and lose a mile.

Most of us rail at losing gained ground. How do we deal with these ornery attackers of productivity?

HOLY CHEESE FRIES!

If I were to have accumulated a dollar for every impediment I've experienced, I'd be wealthy.

Wait. Through the travail, there have been moments I've considered it akin to a four-letter word. I'm not saying "four-letter word" in a derogatory sense, but rather, I'm referring to the frustration that postponement evokes. The intention is not about twiddling our thumbs. It refers to active endurance. Fortunately, it yields constructive fruit; namely, perseverance.

In our fast-paced world of drive-throughs, online ordering, and curbside pickup, we've lost the art of patience. How does that jive with a God who keeps rhythm at an entirely different pace? He is not bound by time and space and is never in a hurry.

Revelation 1:8 describes His Omniscience: "'I am the Alpha and the Omega,' says the Lord God, 'who is and who was and who is to come, the Almighty.'"

Quick fixes, instant gratification, and faster internet has become the norm. Flashback to the days without electricity. Technology has evolved much. We've forgotten how to slow down.

It's only been a short 111 years since the first automobile was built.[232] Cars have improved since that first Model T.

We can liken God to a Crock-Pot in a microwave world.

There was plenty of postponement in the airline industry. Unplanned occurrences cause unwanted delays. Ice, unruly storms, and holding patterns don't adhere to schedules. It was a great place to put forbearance into practice.

I recall a flight to Miami scheduled to arrive at 11:00 p.m. and continue to a nearby city by midnight. A mechanical issue obliged everyone to disembark. Try attaining an open restaurant during the late-night hours.

Grumpy, drowsy bodies grew weary of the extended interval. Our creative impulses kicked in, and we rolled the beverage carts into the lobby.

As a flight attendant, I faced plenty of tough situations. This required much self-control. Despite the long duty day, we were to embody kindness in the midst of anger and frustration. I held my tongue when necessary. There's something about a loud, boisterous voice inches from your nose that makes one want to tee off. Not appropriate.

Have you determined by now that you desire God? Even better, you've chosen to become His son or daughter. Wonderful!

The process of learning to communicate with Him is lifelong. He loves to hear from His kids. But there is much to comprehend about prayer. It is a two-way exchange. Listening is vital. He is alive and able to communicate with mankind.[233]

God's delays don't always mean no. If what we're praying for lines up with His Word, then what should be the reason for postponement? It could be timing. God's ways are perfect. It may not seem so when we don't understand, but He sees the big picture.[234]

A second opinion for the fifth surgery was a wiser choice. Had I not taken the interval of time to seek Him, it might have turned out much worse.

GOD IS NEVER TOO BUSY FOR US, AND HE DOESN'T PLACE US ON HOLD.

He may, however, postpone His response. Our part is to trust He is working on our behalf.[235]

It stretches our faith when prayers go unanswered for years. I've experienced immediate answers and some that I'm still anticipating. We draw closer into fellowship with our Creator as we lean on Him for alleviations.

Sharing our burdens with one another can ease our troubles. Solace is available when we learn of another's struggles. We know we aren't alone. When we come together as a community and reach out beyond ourselves, it reassures. It also encourages our hearts. I've found great satisfaction in knowing God has used my agony to boost another's morale.

Endurance is an essential ingredient for any athlete. A race is not won without proper training and preparation. The spiritual walk is compared to a runner who competes for a prize.[236] The more we persevere, the stronger we become. The battles are won in victory as we stand resilient in the test of trials.[237] Resist the temptation to throw in the towel and have expectation that God will see you through the worst of conditions. He is faithful.[238]

Losing my father in such a dreadful manner knocked me off my rocker. All the petitions and intercession I invested in him seemed to fall by the wayside. Yet as I recognize the undeniable fact he spent his last week with God, I hold the likelihood it wasn't for naught. He returned to his faith in sincerity, and it's my utmost hope he made it home.

Never give up believing for the impossible.

A merry heart does good like medicine.[239] I was on the cusp of a total makeover in my words. Each seed of God's Word spoken revolutionized me. Years of living in His statutes wasn't the same as speaking them out loud. I acquired a whole new disposition.

Moments of sheer exasperation still reared up as I made strides. I would sprint for a while, fall down and skin my knees, and get back up.

Sapped, I longed to close the day. My husband and I stayed overnight at a friend's house while he was on vacation. It was the typical night of three enemas. Singeing angst rebuffed my prospect of slumber. I searched for the clock: 1:00 a.m.

Nearing the end of the unpleasant ordeal, the tube came loose. Water gushed out, soaking my pajamas and the bed.

I stripped the bedding and threw it in the dryer. Mouse droppings exploded everywhere.

The blow dryer in my hand overheated as the dryer buzzed: 2:00 a.m.

My husband snored in the adjoining room.

I gathered the load of sheets and blankets. The lump formed in my throat.

"No. I refuse to cry. No."

Too late. The waterworks didn't heed my message.

"Aww, man. Here it comes."

My frazzled nerves gave in to the impulse. I jutted myself on the bed and sobbed.

Compiled data from medical professionals and extensive research added up to the following conclusion: The concoction of impaired nerves, tangled fascia, and adhesions conglomerated, denying me proper functionality.

"Maybe from now on, I'll just smell food and pretend I ate it. Then I won't pay for it later."

Have you felt battered and bruised by life's gale winds? Lean into God's love and grace. Jesus knows what it feels like to endure the worst of situations. He paved the way for us. We can come to our High Priest who ever lives to make intercession for us.[240]

God presents us with plenty of long-suffering as we grow. He is "merciful and gracious, slow to anger and abundant in loving-kindness and truth."[241]

Digital photos are on-the-spot wonders. Especially in light of the fact that a few spans ago, we used a substance dubbed as film. The negatives were sent off to be developed. What a concept. Explain that to a millennial.

Payphones and an absence of computers fostered bountiful opportunities for a vivid imagination. I posses several scars on my knees to verify I played outside for hours as a youngster.

We're so fortunate that we no longer have to get from place to place by horse or chariot. Our mail structure is, for the most part, quick and effective. What a blessing. We make calls and send texts or e-mails in a matter of seconds.

I remember when researching an idea or subject meant going to the library and checking out a book. Plentiful resources are now at our fingertips.

In spite of our modern conveniences, there will always be days when things don't go our way. The need to grow in mellowness comes in handy. It's useful to realize no amount of technology will bring all the riposte we seek.

Where would I be without the tender mercies of the Lord? I thank Him for carrying me when I was unable to walk through my sorrows. He is there for us and never leaves us when we belong to Him.[242]

DOWN ONE RABBIT HOLE INTO ANOTHER I WENT.

The never-ending process without resolution provided

the ideal environment to give up. It took years of long-suffering and delays to bring me to a place of maturity. I'm still in that process and will continue to be as long as I'm on the earth.

Ponder the idea of planting a seed in the ground. The soil nourishes the small start. Water is provided. The sun's rays give the needed ingredient to bring growth. To cut short this necessary phased progression would result in malfunction.

Our relationship with God will be a series of ups and downs, successes and failures. Mistakes teach us what not to do at the next turn. Hopefully.

I recently had the true awareness of what it means to be smart. A friend and retired English teacher imparted this word of wisdom:

"Sometimes I don't feel smart if I don't know enough about a specific subject," I stated.

"Being smart isn't about knowing everything. It means that you are always learning," she responded.

I like that.

Little by little, my faith for healing grew like a weed. Strange. How is it possible? I lived most of my life as a follower of Christ and missed a critical aspect of faith. The spoken truth out loud shifted my thoughts and outlook.

I persisted in going against the tide of circumstances. Days turned into weeks, then months and years.

Joy consumed me. Confidence bloomed, and expectation blossomed. The fragrance of positivity captivated me in a way I had never experienced before.

Inner transformation precedes outward manifestation. This applies to so many situations.

I continued to go forward at every reputable healing meeting and receive prayer. Reform took root. This stubborn determination for better wouldn't concede. In agonizing moments, I found the capability to praise and thank God regardless of the distress.

Crises can become catalysts of sheer discouragement, or they can foster grit to dig deeper into faith. For myself, there have been both. I forewent my expectation and grabbed hold of His hand. I knew deep down His truths were real. I did the work and invested time and sacrifice in implementing these truths. Simultaneously, all I felt and saw was the same old circumstances. It tried me to my core.

An occurrence of late reflected the conversion that had come about in me.

While I was at the shopping mall, the Holy Spirit prompted me to talk to a specific lady.

"What am I going to say?"

You'd think by now I wouldn't have posed the query to God. The setting wasn't infrequent.

I sauntered her way.

"I know you don't know me, but I'm led to ask if you are okay with me praying for you?"

Turns out she was okay with it. She shared her chronicle of physical concerns.

"From what I gather, we are to thank God after we're healed," she concluded.

"We thank Him now. Worship Him while you wait. He's worthy," I quipped.

What exultation overflowed. Despite all the disturbances, I had assimilated a different mindset. How could I not ponder the grace of God in producing such upbeat conclusions?

Fasting, worshiping, tithing, and so on were a continual part of my armory against defeat. The immense desire to be whole still eluded me. I remained determined to continue in confidence for better.

"You're so steadfast."

I smiled back at my girlfriend. She's seen me through tears and laughter.

"You're so consistent in your faith."

The words spoken meant more to me than she could ever know.

Before this calamity, I'd had a bright future.

High school was my happy place. It was where I dodged all the turmoil at home. I loved being a cheerleader. My amazing classmates voted me prom princess and homecoming queen, an honor I hold dear to this day. It was like oil dripping down a dry cavern. The turbulence at home was undisclosed to many. These sunny gifts decreased my woes and encouraged me. I cherish the wonderful souls who shared my adolescent years in education.

My late teens and early twenties escorted in several paid acting and modeling jobs. I competed in a few pageants, as well. I had scores of dreams and aspirations. The sides blew off. The bottom fell out. The monster of torment sank that ship.

Can I say that there are bouts of remorse for what could have been? No question. Yet I have gained a greater pearl. Knowing the God of creation has far outweighed what I might have achieved.

He loves people and has given me an immense love for them. I would choose Him over all the treasures this world could give.

THE QUESTION IS REAL: WHAT DO YOU DO WHEN YOU'RE DOING EVERYTHING YOU KNOW TO BE RIGHT AND NOT SEEING RESULTS YET?

I'm sure I've cried a river that would flood my ankles.

Words can't convey the intense passion I've held to be cured. My consultations with God have been honest. I've brought my questions before Him plenty. These weren't irreverent or disrespectful comments thrown at a holy God. They are bellows from a wounded heart to a loving Father.

"I'm doing my part to put into practice the wisdom and understanding You have given me," I told Him.

I keep fantasizing, dreaming about, and professing to be on the other side of this malady. It has been a persistent vision in my frontal lobe.

God keeps His promises. I have made the decision to contend for my wholeness regardless of what squeals opposition. The pleasant days that drift my way are reason for abundant joy. I cherish each one more than gold.

I've found answers in the Bible. Morsels of courage leap off the page. They call me to press on.

The Word of God is chock-full of stories of those who have gone before us with similar experiences.[243] Second Corinthians 1:3–4 is a special verse to which I clung with all my might, in expectation that one day I, too, would be a comfort to others who need it themselves.[244]

The passages in Job 41 and 42 are resourceful. They shed light on how we stand before the Ancient of Days and recognize His sovereignty.

I appreciate what Joyce Meyer spoke with regard to this subject:

"Some would say if you didn't get your miracle you didn't have enough faith. Maybe it's that God trusted you enough to go through it to get enough experience to be able to go out and help others."[245]

I choose to believe the latter.

Mother Teresa said, "May God break my heart so completely that the whole world falls in it."[246]

Admittedly, this would be my lofty goal and passion, knowing that it's unlikely in its entirety. However, for the ones whom my broken and fragmented message will touch, I rejoice.

Status and performance were stripped away. I was no longer able to calculate my self-worth in worldly prestige. All the years of giving love and acceptance to others boomeranged my direction. I finally seized the fact that I, too, had immense value. It was no longer defined by position or my father's prior behavior toward me.

Who I was in Christ became the focus. I discovered I am not the sum total of my bank account or the events that have happened to me. My strength now comes from my weakness.[247]

THE BONA-FIDE BREAKTHROUGH BLASTED FORTH IN SUCH AN UNEXPECTED FASHION.

God's Spirit touched me in a way that refreshed my weary soul.[248] Something more significant than what I had been seeking transpired.

I drank in the waterfall of revelation that washed over my emotional gate. The sweet fragrance of His mercy met my weakness, and I was undone. Dawn broke, and the night passed in the darkness of my childhood trauma.

I was finally able to release the real offender. Me.

All the poor choices, sins, and fiascoes that harassed me swept away in the tidal wave of God's acceptance. I had learned from a tender young age to bless others. The giver wasn't extending it to herself.

I knew all along I was forgiven, but I had never been successful in forgiving myself. I tried and failed repeatedly. God made a clear point. He wrote on the sky of my mind that He was not mad at me. All His anger and wrath had been satisfied in the atoning work of His Son on Calvary.

I could now renounce the disappointment of all the unmet expectations I presumed I should be. I was His. And that was enough.

I know God already healed me over two thousand years ago when He took the stripes on His back.[249] This is a certain fact. I still trust in His healing power and believe that it will manifest in my physical body. I cling to His promises as a child clutches their favorite most cherished blanket.

Am I still fighting a few battles? Oh yeah. I still have my moments, for sure. The difference is that I have full assurance God is right there with me and I hold expectation.

For now, I continue to speak faith-filled words over my condition that Jesus is my healer. I also make a point to laugh as often as possible. Laughter is healing. It's good to be able to have humor about ourselves sometimes. After all, no one is perfect—except the Lord.

God sent Jesus into this world to get dirty for us and to take our sins upon Himself. He did this so we could have eternal life and live in heaven with Him forever. He's hoping you'll respond to His request. He's waiting for you with open arms.

ABOUT THE AUTHOR

Wendy can be reached at www.heldbyhim.com.

NOTES

ENDNOTES

CHAPTER ONE

1 Colossians 2:9; Philippians 2:6–8

2 Proverbs 3:5–6

3 www.space.com/33527-how-fast-is-the-earth-moving.html.

4 Matthew 9:1–8; Mark 2:10

5 John 10:30; 14:9–11

6 Matthew 3:17; 17:5; Mark 1:11

CHAPTER TWO

7 John 8:3–4

8 John 8:6

9 John 8:7

10 John 8:9

11 John 8:10

12 John 8:11

13 John 8:11

14 http://doctorwoodhead.com/jesus-fulfilled-the-law-part-ii/.

15 1 Timothy 6:5, Matthew 7:15-20, Matthew 23:1-6

16 Ephesians 4:32

17 Colossians 2:14

18 Philippians 2:3

19 Matthew 15:2

20 Matthew 15:4–5

21 Matthew 15:9 NIV

22 Hebrews 4:15

23 Romans 10:4

24 https://www.biblestudytools.com/dictionaries/bakers-evangeli-cal-dictionary/fatherhood-of-god.html.

25 Isaiah 46:9–10 NKJV

26 https://www.abccolumbia.com/2021/12/31/research-shows-80-of-people-abandon-their-new-years-resolutions-by-february/.

27 Romans 8:2

28 Acts 10:38

29 Luke 10:29–37

30 Mark 7:1–8

31 James 1:27

32 Luke 13:10–13
33 Luke 13:14
34 John 1:14
35 Exodus 25:8
36 Exodus 25:21
37 Exodus 25:22
38 Exodus 37:1, 6
39 James 2:13
40 Isaiah 53:5–6, 10–11; Hebrews 9:15

CHAPTER THREE
41 Release date December 15, 2006, Columbia Pictures, Relativity Media, Overbrook Entertainment, Escape Artists.
42 Luke 3:23
43 https://en.m.wikipedia.org/wiki/Instrument_of_Jesus%27_crucifixion.
44 Matthew 27:26–31
45 Luke 23:34
46 Isaiah 53:5
47 Genesis 1:27
48 Genesis 1:27
49 Exodus 34:6
50 https://www.surgicalassociatesofnorthtexas.com.
51 John 1:11
52 "But God proves His love for us in this: while we were still sinners, Christ died for us" (Romans 5:8 BSB).
53 "O LORD, You have searched me and known me. You know when I sit down and when I rise up; You understand my thought from afar" (Psalm 139:1–2).
54 Psalm 96:6
55 Genesis 1:31 NIV
56 Matthew 5:17
57 "For the law never made anything perfect. But now we have confidence in a better hope, through which we draw near to God" (Hebrews 7:19 NLT).

CHAPTER FOUR
58 Deuteronomy 4:29; Jeremiah 29:13
59 Isaiah 53:1–12
60 Philippians 2:7

61 Luke 1:26–38

62 Hebrews 2:17

63 https://en.m.wikipedia.org/wiki/Disciple_(Christianity).

64 John 1:38

65 https://www.christianity.com/wiki/jesus-christ/why-was-the-messiah-expected-to-free-israel-from-rome.html.

66 Psalm 23:4

67 John 14:9

68 John 14:10

69 1 Peter 1:2

70 John 15:15; James 2:23; Exodus 33:11

71 John 14:27

CHAPTER FIVE

72 Psalm 139:13–15

73 https://www.painscience.com/articles/how-many-muscles.php.

74 https://bodytomy.com/how-many-bones-are-in-human-body.

75 https://sofrep.com/fightersweeep/the-centrifuge-what-its-like-to-pull-gs/.

76 2 Timothy 3:16

77 Psalm 103:8

78 Psalm 69:16

79 Ephesians 2:7

80 Ephesians 4:32

81 Psalm 107:6

82 "If you confess with your mouth Jesus as Lord, and believe in your heart that God raised Him from the dead, you will be saved; for with the heart a person believes, resulting in righteousness, and with the mouth he confesses, resulting in salvation."

83 John 10:10

84 1 Kings 8:23; Micah 7:18; 2 Chronicles 30:9.

85 Proverbs 3:13–20

CHAPTER SIX

86 Genesis 2:9

87 Genesis 3:5 (paraphrased)

88 2 Corinthians 11:14

89 Genesis 3:6

90 Genesis 3:1

91 Genesis 3:2

92 Genesis 3:4–5
93 Genesis 2:17
94 Genesis 3:6
95 Genesis 3:7
96 Genesis 3:22
97 Hebrews 13:8
98 Hebrews 13:5
99 Acts 10:34
100 John 6:37

CHAPTER SEVEN
101 "Trust in the LORD with all your heart and do not lean on your own understanding. In all your ways acknowledge Him and He will make your paths straight."
102 https://billygraham.org/Topics:CrisisSituations,Faith,God.
103 John 10:9–11
104 Matthew 26:53
105 John 10:18
106 Revelation 3:20
107 Matthew 11:28–30
108 Psalm 6:6
109 Psalm 139:17–18
110 Romans 8:28
111 Transcutaneous electrical nerve stimulator

CHAPTER EIGHT
112 https://m.ranker.com/list/desert-phenomena/kellen-perry.
113 Matthew 11:28–30
114 Revelation 21:4
115 Luke 12:7
116 Numbers 23:19
117 Luke 12:15
118 Matthew 7:7–11
119 Philippians 2:5–11
120 https://www.merriamwebster.com/dictionary/humility.
121 "Let each of you look not only to his own interests, but also to the interests of others" (Philippians 2:4 ESV).

CHAPTER NINE
122 www.philvaz.com/apologetics/a106.html.

123 https://www.gotquestions.org/definition-ekklesia.html.
124 https://www.dictionary.com/browse/organism.
125 https://quizlet.com/373619157/what-is-an-organization-flash-cards/.
126 Mark 2:16
127 Romans 12:4–8
128 https://www.oxfordlearnersdictionaries.com/us/definition/english/hypocrite.
129 Psalm 18:30
130 Philippians 2:13
131 John 18:10
132 John 21:21
133 John 21:22
134 1 Corinthians 15:32 CEB
135 Mark 16:19
136 Matthew 27:62–66
137 John 11:25
138 evidence.https://www.sciencedirect.com/science/article/pii/0168583X87902333, https://digitalcommons.liberty.edu/cgi/viewcontent.cgi?article=1026&context=Its_fac_pubs.
139 YouTube: Shroud of Turin Used to Create 3D Copy of Jesus.
140 Isaiah 53:5
141 Psalm 86:5; Psalm 145:9; Luke 6:36; Titus 3:5
142 Psalm 136:1 NKJV
143 1 Peter 2:24
144 1 Peter 4:12
145 Romans 8:26

CHAPTER TEN

146 https://www.britannica.com/science/human-body.
147 https://www.heartmath.com/science/.
148 https://innovativemedicine.com/a-scientific-comprehension-of-body-mind-and-spirit/.
149 https://blog.biblesforamerica.org/the-three-parts-of-man-spirit-soul-and-body/.
150 Genesis 2:7
151 Acts 10:34–35
152 Hebrews 4:14–16
153 Romans 5:12
154 https://bible.knowing-jesus.com/topics/Missing-The-Mark.

155 Colossians 1:16–17
156 Revelation 12:9 ESV
157 Genesis 3:1; Ephesians 6:12
158 Matthew 4:1–2
159 Matthew 4:4
160 Matthew 4:6–7
161 Matthew 4:8–9
162 https://www.gty.org/library/sermons-library/90-84/the-tempta-tion-of-christ.
163 1 Corinthians 15:45–48
164 John 3:16
165 1 Peter 1:18–19
166 Hebrews 4:15
167 Philippians 2:6–8
168 Matthew 26:39
169 Matthew 26:53–54
170 2 Corinthians 5:19
171 Jeremiah 29:11
172 Matthew 8:23–27
173 https://www.challies.com/articles/counterfeit-detection-part-1/.
174 Matthew 4:1–11; Luke 4:1–13
175 Genesis 3:1
176 Luke 22:3
177 John 8:44
178 2 Timothy 1:7
179 James 1:13
180 1 John 1:5
181 Luke 24:39; Ephesians 1:20
182 Hebrews 1:14
183 Genesis 19:1; 19:15; 28:12; 32:1
184 Genesis 3:6–7
185 Ezekiel 28:13–19
186 Revelation 12:3
187 Isaiah 14:12 KJV
188 Ephesians 6:12
189 Revelation 12:10
190 John 10:10
191 Matthew 4:3; 1 Thessalonians 3:5
192 Revelation 12:9
193 1 Peter 5:8

194 Job 1:6–12
195 Job 1:7
196 Isaiah 9:6
197 Isaiah 40:3–5
198 Isaiah 7:14
199 Isaiah 52:13–53:12
200 Isaiah 14:13–15
201 Isaiah 46:9–10 NIV
202 Job 40–41
203 Matthew 1:20–23
204 Zechariah 3:1
205 Revelation 12:7–9
206 Genesis 1:31
207 Romans 11:33–35
208 https://billygraham.org/answer/people-often-call-christianity-a-bloody-religion-but-ignore-the-atrocities-in-world-religion-why-is-this/.
209 Hebrews 9:22
210 1 Peter 1:19
211 Colossians 2:13–14
212 John 14:6
213 Isaiah 53:4–7
214 https://www.crosswalk.com/faith/bible-study/what-is-the-meaning-of-metanoia-and-its-biblical-signifigance.html?amp=1.
215 John14:9; 2 Corinthians 5:21
216 1 Peter 2:24; Romans 3:21–26
217 Galatians 5:1
218 https://www.crosswalk.com/faith/bible-study/what-does-selah-mean.html.
219 http://www.cbn.com/spirituallife/onlinediscipleship/easter/A_Physician's_View_of_the_Crucifixion_of_Jesus_Christ.aspx.
220 1 Peter 1:19–20
221 John 19:1
222 www.cbcg.org/scourging-crucifixion.html.
223 2 Corinthians 5:21
224 1 John 2:2
225 John 11:25–26; Mark 16:6; 1 Thessalonians 4:14; Luke 24:6–7; 1 Peter 1:3; Matthew 28:5–6; 2 Corinthians 5:14–15; 1 Corinthians 15:21; 15:3–4; Matthew 20:18–19; John 20:8–9
226 https://www.namb.net/apologetics/resource/josephus-and-jesus/.

227 https://coldcasechristianity.com/writings/is-there-any-evidence-for-jesus-outside-the-bible/.
228 Colossians 2:15
229 1 Corinthians 15:12–19
230 John 16:13–14
231 John 14:15–27

CHAPTER ELEVEN
232 https://en.wikipedia.org/wiki/Ford_Model_T.
233 Deuteronomy 5:24
234 Isaiah 46:10
235 John 5:17
236 1 Corinthians 9:24
237 James 1:12
238 1 Peter 5:10
239 Proverbs 17:22 NKJV
240 Hebrews 7:25
241 Psalm 86:15
242 Deuteronomy 31:8
243 1 Peter 4:12–14
244 "Blessed be the God and Father of our Lord Jesus Christ, the Father of mercies and God of all comfort, who comforts us in all our affliction so that we will be able to comfort those who are in any affliction with the comfort with which we ourselves are comforted by God."
245 Joni table talk unshakable trust.
246 https://www.goodreads.com/quotes/204308-may-god-break-my-heart-so-completely-that-the-whole.
247 2 Corinthians 12:9–10
248 Matthew 11:28–30
249 Isaiah 53:5